BOLLINGEN SERIES LII

Pandora (Anesidora) between Pallas Athene and Hephaestus
(The Blade Kylix)

PANDORA'S BOX

The Changing Aspects of a

Mythical Symbol

By

DORA and ERWIN PANOFSKY

BOLLINGEN SERIES LII

PRINCETON UNIVERSITY PRESS

Published by Princeton University Press, 41 William Street,
Princeton, New Jersey 08540
In the United Kingdom: Princeton University Press, Oxford

Library of Congress Card No. 55-11598
ISBN 0-691-09809-3 (hardback)
ISBN 0-691-01824-3 (paperback)
First PRINCETON/BOLLINGEN PAPERBACK printing, 1978
First Paperback printing in the Mythos Series, 1991

THIS IS NUMBER LII IN BOLLINGEN SERIES
SPONSORED BY BOLLINGEN FOUNDATION

Princeton University Press books are printed on acid-free paper,
and meet the guidelines for permanence and durability of the
Committee on Production Guidelines for Book Longevity of the
Council on Library Resources

10   9   8   7   6   5   4   3   2   (pbk.)

Printed in the United States of America

IN MEMORIAM

GUSTAV PAULI

MYTHOS

The Princeton/Bollingen Series in World Mythology

Contents

List of Illustrations

Preface

THERE is a strange fascination about a mythological character that has retained its vitality up to our own day and, in the course of time, has lent its name to English queens as well as to French policemen, to the philosopher's stone as well as to a gang of fifteen-year-old murderers in Philadelphia.[1]

Succumbing to this fascination, we have attempted not so much to give a complete monograph on Pandora as to pursue a number of special problems into whatever corners they happened to lead us. But, even so, the subject proved to be so complex that the major portion of this Preface must consist of a list of those who generously helped us with advice, suggestions, information, and, last but not least, generous assistance in obtaining photographs: Mr. W. Andrews, Mr. S. D. Cleveland, Mr. M. Davies, Dr. O. Demus, Dr. H. Diepolder, Mme Jeanne Dupic, Professor H. von Erffa, Professor H. Fränkel, Professor T. W. Furniss, Dr. H. Gerson, Miss Meta Harrsen, Professor W. S. Heckscher, Professor J. S. Held, Mr. Philip Hofer, Professor E. H. Kantorowicz, Miss Ida Kapp, Professor J. F. Kienitz, Professor P. O. Kristeller, Professor E. E. Lowinsky, Mr. E. I. Musgrave, Dr. Carl Nordenfalk, Dr. K. T. Parker, Professor Charles P. Parkhurst, Dr. J. Q. van Regteren Altena, Mlle Madeleine Rocher Jauneau, Professor H. O. Schwarz, Professor E. Sjöquist, Professor W. Stechow, and Professor H. van de Waal.

[1] *Evening Bulletin* (Philadelphia), November 4, 1954. The persistent popularity of Pandora and the great variety of connotations attached to her name are evidenced by the fact that the Manhattan telephone directory lists the following firms: Pandora Frocks, Inc., Pandora Interiors, Pandora Knitwear Co., Pandora Novelty Co., and Jewels by Pandora, Inc. A coffee shop called "Pandora's Box" may be found at Barrow and Fourth Streets, in Greenwich Village. When the United States Department of State decided to publish the papers of the Yalta Conference, a cartoon, entitled "Pandora," was published in the Philadelphia *Evening Bulletin* of March 19, 1955, and reprinted in the *New York Times*, March 20, 1955, Section 4, p. E5; it shows the Department of State in the guise of Pandora, frightened by the demons escaping from the "box" just opened by her, the representational type still remotely related to Hammatt Billings' woodcut reproduced in our *fig. 58.*

To all of these we are much indebted; but our especial gratitude is due to a number of friends and colleagues whose patience we have tried over and over again: Dr. Paul Coremans, Professor Harold F. Cherniss, Professor J. G. van Gelder, and Mr. John S. Summerson, curator of Sir John Soane's Museum, London. Where we have been able to remember individual contributions, we have acknowledged this fact in the proper places; where our memory has failed us, we ask all our informants to accept our apologies together with our thanks.

DORA AND ERWIN PANOFSKY

Princeton, New Jersey
October 15, 1955

Preface to the Second Edition

Thanks to the co-operative spirit of the publishers, the present reprint of our little book could be transformed into a second, revised edition. We were given the opportunity not only to correct a considerable number of typographical and factual errors (among them a silly confusion of Phidias' *Parthenos* with the same artist's *Zeus*)* but also to add a further section of addenda, provided with seven new illustrations (pp. 142 ff., *figs. 61–67*). These addenda contain supplementary information that became available to us through books and articles published after 1956 or previously overlooked by us, through further research, and through private communications. The sources of this supplementary information are indicated in their proper place; but we wish to repeat here our thanks to all those who encouraged and assisted us by their friendly interest.

Princeton, October 1961   DORA AND ERWIN PANOFSKY

---

* See p. 9. This confusion was pointed out by at least one reviewer and, *in litteris*, by several friends. Other substantive (as opposed to purely typographical) changes have been made on pp. 59, 74–76, 102, 105, and 108 f., as well as in the corresponding columns of the index.

PANDORA'S BOX

The Changing Aspects of a Mythical Symbol

I

Pandora in the Medieval Tradition

No MYTH is more familiar than that of Pandora, none perhaps has been so completely misunderstood. Pandora is the first woman, the beautiful mischief; she opens a forbidden box, out comes every evil that flesh is heir to; hope only remains. The box of Pandora is proverbial, and that is the more remarkable as she never had a box at all." [1]

This statement, made by Jane Harrison more than fifty years ago, is no less valid today than it was then.[2] There are, however, several things about Pandora that even now require investigation. Why is it that she became famous on account of an attribute that was neither a box nor properly hers? How can we explain that she, in contrast to so many other mythological characters, never appears in medieval art and accomplished her revival—in fact, a real renaissance—on French rather than Italian soil? And, while untold numbers of books and essays have been devoted to her role in Greek religion,

---

[1] J. E. Harrison, "Pandora's Box," *Journal of Hellenic Studies*, XX, 1900, pp. 99 ff. For general information and further literature, see the comprehensive survey in Pauly-Wissowa, *Real-encyclopädie der klassischen Altertumswissenschaft*, XVIII, 3, 1949, cols. 529 ff. (W. M. Oldfather); cf. also Roscher, *Ausführliches Lexikon der griechischen und römischen Mythologie*, III, 1887–1902, cols. 1524 ff. (P. Weizsäcker) and 3045 ff. (K. Bapp, *s.v.* "Prometheus").

[2] Even Schopenhauer (referred to in n. 6, p. 7), though fully familiar with the Greek sources, speaks of Pandora's *Büchse*; for more recent lapses in equally respectable circles, see Pauly-Wissowa, *op. cit.*, XVIII, 3, col. 538. An amusing reversal of the historical process is found in R. Petsch, "Die Kunstform von Goethes 'Pandora,'" *Die Antike*, VI, 1930, pp. 15 ff.: ". . . in dem er [Goethe] aus der schauervollen Büchse der Pandora, von der die alte Sage erzählte, ein wundervoll geformtes Gefäss macht . . ." (p. 27).

art, and literature as well as to her significance in Goethe's play named after her,[3] what do we know of what happened to her in between?

In an attempt to answer these questions we shall not dwell on such moot problems as whether Pandora was originally an earth goddess (so that her name should be interpreted as "the all-giver" rather than "the all-gifted"); whether she opened her vessel in imitation of the daughters of Cecrops, who improvidently lifted the lid off the basket containing the little Erichthonius; or whether her πιθοιγία reflects a ritual connected with the Greek equivalent of Halloween, the Anthesteria feast. Nor shall we try to dispel the obscurity that surrounds the *locus classicus*, Hesiod's famous account of the Pandora story in his *Works and Days*[4] (supplemented by a shorter passage in the

[3] For essays on the interpretation of Goethe's Pandora, see the list in Pauly-Wissowa, *ibidem*, col. 531, unfortunately omitting the most satisfactory contribution: E. Cassirer, "Goethes Pandora," first published in *Zeitschrift für Aesthetik und allgemeine Kunstwissenschaft*, XIII, 1919, pp. 113 ff.; reprinted in *Idee und Gestalt*, Berlin, 1st edition, 1921, and *Freiheit und Form*, Berlin, 1st edition, 1922. The good analysis in K. Viëtor, *Goethe*, Bern [1949], pp. 196–204, appeared too late to be included in Pauly-Wissowa. See also below, pp. 122 ff.

[4] Hesiod, *Works and Days*, lines 57–101 (here, for the sake of convenience, reprinted from H. G. Evelyn-White's edition in the Loeb Classical Library, Cambridge, 1950, pp. 6 ff.):

τοῖς δ' ἐγὼ ἀντὶ πυρὸς δώσω κακόν, ᾧ κεν ἅπαντες
τέρπωνται κατὰ θυμὸν ἐὸν κακὸν ἀμφαγαπῶντες.
Ὣς ἔφατ'· ἐκ δ' ἐγέλασσε πατὴρ ἀνδρῶν τε θεῶν τε.
60 Ἥφαιστον δ' ἐκέλευσε περικλυτὸν ὅττι τάχιστα
γαῖαν ὕδει φύρειν, ἐν δ' ἀνθρώπου θέμεν αὐδὴν
καὶ σθένος, ἀθανάτῃς δὲ θεῇς εἰς ὦπα ἐίσκειν
παρθενικῆς καλὸν εἶδος ἐπήρατον· αὐτὰρ Ἀθήνην
ἔργα διδασκῆσαι, πολυδαίδαλον ἱστὸν ὑφαίνειν·
65 καὶ χάριν ἀμφιχέαι κεφαλῇ χρυσέην Ἀφροδίτην
καὶ πόθον ἀργαλέον καὶ γυιοκόρους μελεδώνας·
ἐν δὲ θέμεν κύνεόν τε νόον καὶ ἐπίκλοπον ἦθος
Ἑρμείην ἤνωγε, διάκτορον Ἀργεϊφόντην.
Ὣς ἔφαθ'· οἳ δ' ἐπίθοντο Διὶ Κρονίωνι ἄνακτι.
70 αὐτίκα δ' ἐκ γαίης πλάσσεν κλυτὸς Ἀμφιγυήεις
παρθένῳ αἰδοίῃ ἴκελον Κρονίδεω διὰ βουλάς·

"But I will give men as the price for fire an evil thing in which they may all be glad of heart while they embrace their own destruction."

So said the father of men and gods, and laughed aloud. And he bade famous Hephaestus make haste and mix earth with water and to put in it the voice and strength of human kind, and fashion a sweet, lovely maidenshape, like to the immortal goddesses in face; and Athene to teach her needlework and the weaving of the varied web; and golden Aphrodite to shed grace upon her head and cruel longing and cares that weary the limbs. And he charged Hermes the guide, the Slayer of Argus, to put in her a shameless mind and a deceitful nature.

So he ordered. And they obeyed the lord Zeus the son of Cronos. Forthwith the famous Lame God moulded clay in the likeness of a modest maid, as the son of Cronos purposed. And the goddess bright-eyed Athene girded and clothed her, and the divine Graces and

ζῶσε δὲ καὶ κόσμησε θεὰ γλαυκῶπις
    Ἀθήνη·
ἀμφὶ δέ οἱ Χάριτές τε θεαὶ καὶ
    πότνια Πειθὼ
ὅρμους χρυσείους ἔθεσαν χροΐ· ἀμφὶ
    δὲ τήν γε
75 Ὧραι καλλίκομοι στέφον ἄνθεσιν
    εἰαρινοῖσιν·
[πάντα δέ οἱ χροΐ κόσμον ἐφήρμοσε
    Παλλὰς Ἀθήνη.]
ἐν δ' ἄρα οἱ στήθεσσι διάκτορος
    Ἀργεϊφόντης
Ψεύδεά θ' αἱμυλίους τε λόγους καὶ
    ἐπίκλοπον ἦθος
[τεῦξε Διὸς βουλῆσι βαρυκτύπου· ἐν δ'
    ἄρα φωνὴν]
80 θῆκε θεῶν κῆρυξ, ὀνόμηνε δὲ τήνδε
    γυναῖκα
Πανδώρην, ὅτι πάντες Ὀλύμπια δώματ'
    ἔχοντες
δῶρον ἐδώρησαν, πῆμ' ἀνδράσιν
    ἀλφηστῇσιν.
Αὐτὰρ ἐπεὶ δόλον αἰπὺν ἀμήχανον
    ἐξετέλεσσεν,
εἰς Ἐπιμηθέα πέμπε πατὴρ κλυτὸν
    Ἀργεϊφόντην
85 δῶρον ἄγοντα, θεῶν ταχὺν ἄγγελον· οὐδ'
    Ἐπιμηθεὺς
ἐφράσαθ', ὥς οἱ ἔειπε Προμηθεὺς μή ποτε
    δῶρον
δέξασθαι πὰρ Ζηνὸς Ὀλυμπίου, ἀλλ'
    ἀποπέμπειν
ἐξοπίσω, μή πού τι κακὸν θνητοῖσι
    γένηται.
αὐτὰρ ὃ δεξάμενος, ὅτε δὴ κακὸν εἶχ',
    ἐνόησεν.
90 Πρὶν μὲν γὰρ ζώεσκον ἐπὶ χθονὶ φῦλ'
    ἀνθρώπων
νόσφιν ἄτερ τε κακῶν καὶ ἄτερ χαλεποῖο
    πόνοιο
νούσων τ' ἀργαλέων, αἵ τ' ἀνδράσι Κῆρας
    ἔδωκαν.
[αἶψα γὰρ ἐν κακότητι βροτοὶ
    καταγηράσκουσιν.]
ἀλλὰ γυνὴ χείρεσσι πίθου μέγα πῶμ'
    ἀφελοῦσα
95 ἐσκέδασ'· ἀνθρώποισι δ' ἐμήσατο κήδεα
    λυγρά.
μούνη δ' αὐτόθι Ἐλπὶς ἐν ἀρρήκτοισι
    δόμοισιν
ἔνδον ἔμιμνε πίθου ὑπὸ χείλεσιν, οὐδὲ
    θύραζε
ἐξέπτη· πρόσθεν γὰρ ἐπέλλαβε πῶμα
    πίθοιο
[αἰγιόχου βουλῇσι Διὸς νεφεληγερέταο.]
100 ἄλλα δὲ μυρία λυγρὰ κατ' ἀνθρώπους
    ἀλάληται·
πλείη μὲν γὰρ γαῖα κακῶν, πλείη δὲ
    θάλασσα·

queenly Persuasion put necklaces of gold upon her, and the rich-haired Hours crowned her head with spring flowers. And Pallas Athene bedecked her form with all manner of finery. Also the Guide, the Slayer of Argus, contrived within her lies and crafty words and a deceitful nature at the will of loud thundering Zeus, and the Herald of the gods put speech in her. And he called this woman Pandora, because all they who dwelt on Olympus gave each a gift, a plague to men who eat bread.

But when he had finished the sheer, hopeless snare, the Father sent glorious Argus-Slayer, the swift messenger of the gods, to take it to Epimetheus as a gift. And Epimetheus did not think on what Prometheus had said to him, bidding him never take a gift of Olympian Zeus, but to send it back for fear it might prove to be something harmful to men. But he took the gift, and afterwards, when the evil thing was already his, he understood.

For ere this the tribes of men lived on earth remote and free from ills and hard toil and heavy sicknesses which bring the Fates upon men; for in misery men grow old quickly. But the woman took off the great lid of the jar with her hands and scattered all these and her thought caused sorrow and mischief to men. Only Hope remained there in an unbreakable home within under the rim of the great jar, and did not fly out at the door; for ere that, the lid of the jar stopped her, by the will of Aegis-holding Zeus who gathers the clouds. But the rest, countless plagues, wander amongst men; for earth is full of evils and the sea is full.

Theogony),[5] which has challenged the ingenuity of the interpreters for more than two thousand years. We incline to believe, with Schopenhauer and a goodly number of recent scholars, that the Fifty-eighth Fable of Babrius, where man as such (ἄνθρωπος) takes the place of Pandora and the vessel contains goods rather than evils, more clearly reflects the original sense of the myth than does the version forced upon posterity by Hesiod;[6] but this, we recognize, is not for art historians to decide.

[5] Hesiod, *Theogony*, lines 570–590 (Evelyn-White, *op. cit.*, pp. 120 ff.) :

570 αὐτίκα δ' ἀντὶ πυρὸς τεῦξεν κακὸν
      ἀνθρώποισιν·
   γαίης γὰρ σύμπλασσε περικλυτὸς
      Ἀμφιγυήεις
   παρθένῳ αἰδοίῃ ἴκελον Κρονίδεω διὰ
      βουλάς.
   ζῶσε δὲ καὶ κόσμησε θεὰ γλαυκῶπις
      Ἀθήνη
   ἀργυφέῃ ἐσθῆτι· κατὰ κρῆθεν δὲ
      καλύπτρην
575 δαιδαλέην χείρεσσι κατέσχεθε, θαῦμα
      ἰδέσθαι·
   [ἀμφὶ δέ οἱ στεφάνους, νεοθηλέος
      ἄνθεα ποίης,
   ἱμερτοὺς περίθηκε καρήατι Παλλὰς
      Ἀθήνη.]
   ἀμφὶ δέ οἱ στεφάνην χρυσέην κεφαλῆφιν
      ἔθηκε,
   τὴν αὐτὸς ποίησε περικλυτὸς
      Ἀμφιγυήεις
580 ἀσκήσας παλάμῃσι, χαριζόμενος Διὶ
      πατρί.
   τῇ δ' ἐνὶ δαίδαλα πολλὰ τετεύχατο,
      θαῦμα ἰδέσθαι,
   κνώδαλ', ὅσ' ἤπειρος πολλὰ τρέφει ἠδὲ
      θάλασσα,
   τῶν ὅ γε πόλλ' ἐνέθηκε,—χάρις δ'
      ἀπελάμπετο πολλή,—
   θαυμάσια, ζῴοισιν ἐοικότα φωνήεσσιν.
585 Αὐτὰρ ἐπεὶ δὴ τεῦξε καλὸν κακὸν
      ἀντ' ἀγαθοῖο,
   ἐξάγαγ', ἔνθα περ ἄλλοι ἔσαν θεοὶ ἠδ'
      ἄνθρωποι,
   κόσμῳ ἀγαλλομένην γλαυκώπιδος
      ὀβριμοπάτρης.
   θαῦμα δ' ἔχ' ἀθανάτους τε θεοὺς
      θνητούς τ' ἀνθρώπους,
   ὡς εἶδον δόλον αἰπύν, ἀμήχανον
      ἀνθρώποισιν.
590 Ἐκ τῆς γὰρ γένος ἐστὶ γυναικῶν
      θηλυτεράων.

Forthwith he made an evil thing for men as the price of fire; for the very famous Limping God formed of earth the likeness of a shy maiden as the son of Cronos willed. And the goddess bright-eyed Athene girded and clothed her with silvery raiment, and down from her head she spread with her hands a broidered veil, a wonder to see; and she, Pallas Athene, put about her head lovely garlands, flowers of new-grown herbs. Also she put upon her head a crown of gold which the very famous Limping God made himself and worked with his own hands as a favour to Zeus his father. On it was much curious work, wonderful to see; for of the many creatures which the land and sea rear up, he put most upon it, wonderful things, like living beings with voices: and great beauty shone out from it.

But when he had made the beautiful evil to be the price for the blessing, he brought her out, delighting in the finery which the bright-eyed daughter of a mighty father had given her, to the place where the other gods and men were. And wonder took hold of the deathless gods and mortal men when they saw that which was sheer guile, not to be withstood by men.

For from her is the race of women and female kind.

[6] See Pauly-Wissowa, *op. cit.*, XVIII, 3, especially cols. 533, 540 ff. Schopenhauer's analysis is

We shall, instead, begin with a brief summary of the factual and, from our point of view, relevant statements made about Pandora in Greek literature. First, Pandora was the image of a beautiful woman, formed of earth and water either by Prometheus, the maker of all men (this according to what seems to be the earliest tradition); or, at the instigation of a vengeful Zeus, by Hephaestus (this according to Hesiod and those dependent on him). Second, this image was animated either by Athena or—with the aid of the fire stolen from heaven—by Prometheus himself, and was perfected by all the other gods, each of whom contributed an appropriate gift (hence the name "Pandora"); and since the gifts of Aphrodite and Hermes were harmful rather than beneficial, the final product turned out to be a καλὸν κακόν, a "beautiful evil." [7] Third, Pandora was conveyed to earth by Hermes and accepted as a wife by Epimetheus, Prometheus' brother, in spite of the latter's warnings; she thus became the mother of all women. [8] Fourth, while living with Epimetheus, she brought upon the world illness and vice by opening a fateful vessel the contents of which, with the exception of Hope, immediately flew away; according to Hesiod and nearly all others, it had originally contained all evils; according to Babrius and a less noted writer, Macedonius the Consul, [9] all goods; but never, so far as we know, a balanced mixture of both. Fifth, this vessel is invariably designated as a πίθος (*dolium* in Latin), a huge earthenware storage jar used for the preservation of wine, oil, and other provisions, and often large enough to serve as a receptacle for the dead or,

found in *Parerga und Paralipomena* (*Mythologische Betrachtungen*), § 200. For the text of Babrius' fable, see n. 13, p. 8; for an illustration of it, *fig. 39*.

[7] Hesiod, *Theogony*, 585. Nonnos, *Dionysiaca*, VII, 58, has γλυκερὸν κακόν; Gregory of Nazianzus (cf. n. 26, p. 12) has τερπωλὴ ὀλοή.

[8] Hesiod, *Theogony*, 590. According to the most widely accepted version, Pyrrha, the daughter of Epimetheus and Pandora, became the wife of Deucalion, and when these two, sole survivors of the Flood, threw stones to be transformed into human beings, the stones thrown by Deucalion became males, those thrown by Pyrrha, females. The notion that Deucalion was the son of Pandora and Prometheus seems to survive only in Hellanonikos' *Scholia in Apollodorum Rhodium* and Strabo.

[9] Macedonius Consul, Epigram no. 71 (*Greek Anthology*, III, p. 92; Loeb Classical Library, IV, p. 41): "I smile when I look on the picture of Pandora's jar, and do not find it was the woman's fault but is due to the Goods' having wings. For as they flutter to Olympus after visiting every region of the world, they ought to fall on the earth too. The woman, after taking off the lid, grew pale-faced, and has lost the splendor of her former charm. Our present life has suffered two losses: woman is grown old and the jar has nothing in it."

later on, a shelter for the living; the very lid that prevents Hope from escaping is described as "big" (μέγα πῶμα). Sixth, this pithos ("kein Transportgefäss") [10] is never represented as a personal possession of Pandora, brought down by her from Mount Olympus; rather it is taken for granted as forming part of her and Epimetheus' domestic establishment, so to speak; [11] one author, Philodemus of Gadara, goes as far as to attribute the act of unsealing it to the husband and not to the wife. [12] Seventh, the motive of this act is, with one exception, left undefined. Curiosity may be implied by all writers (although no formal injunction against the opening of the vessel seems to be mentioned in any classical source); but it is only Babrius, conceiving of the myth not as a story of feminine frailty but as a comment on man's tragic choice between knowledge and contentment, who makes an explicit statement: "Zeus assembled all the goods in the vessel and gave it sealed to man; but man, unable to restrain his eagerness to know, said, 'What in the world can be inside?' And, lifting the lid, he set them free to return to the houses of the gods and to fly thither, thus fleeing heavenwards from the earth. Hope alone remained." [13]

---

[10] H. Fränkel, "Drei Interpretationen aus Hesiod," *Festschrift Richard Reitzenstein*, Göttingen, 1931, pp. 17 ff. For the definition, size, and shape of a pithos, see Pauly-Wissowa, *op. cit.*, v, cols. 1284 ff., and Daremberg-Saglio, *Dictionnaire des antiquités grecques et romaines*, II, 1, Paris, 1892, pp. 332 ff. (*s.v.* "dolium," with illustrations).

[11] According to some authors the pithos was sent to Epimetheus by Zeus; and, according to a humorous variant ascribed to either Aeschylus or Sophocles in recent scholarship, satyrs at first delivered it to Prometheus, who, however, deposited it with Epimetheus with the injunction not to let Pandora into the house (Pauly-Wissowa, *op. cit.*, XVIII, 1, cols. 534 f.). Since this variant seems to be transmitted exclusively by Proclus in his commentary on Hesiod, the Byzantine scholar Johannes Tzetzes composed the following couplet:

Πίθους δ'ὁ Πρόκλος ψευσμάτων πεπλησμένους
πάλιν παράγει, καὶ σατύρους, καὶ κρότους.

(T. Gaisford, *Poetae Minores Graeci*, IV, Oxford, 1820, p. 87.)

[12] Philodemus, Περὶ εὐσεβείας, 130, referred to in Pauly-Wissowa, *op. cit.*, VI, 1909, p. 182, and Roscher, *op. cit.*, I, 1884–1886, col. 1284.

[13] *Babrii Fabulae Aesopeae*, 58 (O. Crusius, ed., Leipzig, 1897, pp. 53 f.) :

Ζεὺς ἐν πίθῳ τὰ χρηστὰ πάντα συλλέξας
ἔθηκεν αὐτὸν πωμάσας παρ' ἀνθρώπῳ.
ὁ δ' ἀκρατὴς ἄνθρωπος εἰδέναι σπεύδων
τί ποτ' ἦν ἐν αὐτῷ, καὶ τὸ πῶμα κινήσας,
διῆκ' ἀπελθεῖν αὐτὰ πρὸς θεῶν οἴκους,
κἀκεῖ πέτεσθαι τῆς τε γῆς ἄνω φεύγειν.
μόνη δ' ἔμεινεν ἐλπίς. . .

Evidently this version is just as logical as Hesiod's is not. With Babrius, that which is inside the vessel (the goods) remains available to man, while that which escapes from it is lost to him; by opening it, he forfeits the goods but retains hope. With Hesiod, only that which escapes from the vessel (the evils) gains power over man; so that hope, remaining within, could not have any influence on him. This is obviously the opposite of what Hesiod meant to convey, no matter whether he conceived of hope as evil, good, or neutral.

As regards the Latin classics, the evidence is surprisingly scanty. Pandora—and this may be one of the reasons why the Italians never felt at home with her—does not appear in either Ovid or Virgil, Horace or Lucan, Cicero or Seneca, Martianus Capella or Macrobius. In fact, her name is mentioned by only four Roman writers, and only one of these obscurely and briefly alludes to the pithos incident.

Pliny records, as does Pausanias, that the base of Phidias' *Parthenos* at Athens showed the "Creation of [more precisely: The Bestowal of Gifts upon] Pandora with Twenty Gods Present," and he reveals a characteristic unfamiliarity with the subject by using Greek instead of Latin words (*Pandoras genesim* rather than *Pandorae originem* or *formationem*) as well as by stressing the fact that he is merely quoting (*appellant*).[14] Hyginus says only that, after Prometheus had shaped the first man out of clay, Vulcan, at the behest of Jupiter, produced the image of a woman, also of clay, "to whom Minerva gave a soul, while each of the other gods gave her another present, wherefore she was called Pandora"; and that "she was given as a wife to Epimetheus, Prometheus' brother."[15] Fulgentius, ascribing Pandora's creation to Prometheus rather than Vulcan, translates her Greek name as *omnium munus* (or, in another passage, *universale munus*) and adds a succinct allegorical explanation: she was so named "quod anima sit omnium munus generale," "because the soul is the general gift of all."[16] In another chapter, however, dealing with the birth of Erichthonius, he confuses her with Pandrosus, one of the daughters of Cecrops.[17] The only Roman writer to mention the pithos motif is Porphyrio, the third-century commentator on Horace;

[14] Pliny, *Naturalis historia*, XXXVI, 5, 4: "In basi autem quod caelatum est *Pandoras genesim* appellant; di sunt nascentes [should read: *nascenti adstantes*] xx numero." For reflections of this composition in art, see H. Schrader, *Phidias*, Frankfurt, 1924, pp. 296 ff.; cf. also, as a parallel, the big London krater illustrated, e.g., in Roscher, *op. cit.*, III, cols. 1527–28.

[15] Hyginus, *Fabulae*, 142: "Prometheus Iapeti filius primus homines ex luto finxit. Postea Vulcanus Iovis iussu ex luto mulieris effigiem fecit, cui Minerva animam dedit, ceterique dii alius aliud donum dederunt; ob id Pandoram nominarunt. Ea data in coniugium Epimetheo fratri, inde nata est Pyrrha. . . ."

[16] Fulgentius, *Mythologiae*, 46, 82: "Denique [Prometheus] Pandoram dicitur formasse; Pandora enim Graece dicitur omnium munus, quod anima munus sit omnium generale"; *ibidem*, 52, 89: "Pandora enim universale munus dicitur."

[17] *Ibidem*, 51, 88.

divagating upon *Carmina* I, 3, 29, he says: "Hesiodus ait, cum ignis a caelo furto Promethei subductus esset, Pandoram inmissam terris poenae causa; nam per eam mulierem patefacto dolio erupisse pestium genera, quibus homines laborarent" [18] ("Hesiod says that, when Prometheus had stolen the fire from heaven, Pandora was sent to earth as a punishment; for, when this woman had opened a storage jar, all kinds of plagues from which mankind suffers burst forth").

This, then, is all the mythographers of the Latin Middle Ages [19] could know about Pandora. What they in fact did know about her (Porphyrio apparently remaining unnoticed) was largely limited to Fulgentius. An early protohumanist such as Baudri de Bourgueil (1046–1130) could condense the high-medieval concept of Pandora into one badly scanned but unequivocally complimentary distich:

> *"Pandora" dicta fuit quam fecit imago Prometheus,*
> *Cunctorum munus et generale bonum.* [20]

The brief account in Boccaccio's *Genealogia deorum*, though based upon the same Fulgentius text and as silent about the pithos story as are the other medieval sources, [21] speaks less kindly of Pandora. Always pretending to

---

[18] *Porphyrionis Commentarii in Horatium* (S. Meyer, ed., Leipzig, 1874, p. 7). We are indebted for this reference, which tends to be overlooked in recent writing, to Dr. Ida Kapp.
[19] The "Mythographus II" retells the Erichthonius story, with Pandora substituted for Pandrosus, as told by Fulgentius, in two different passages, 37 and 40 (Bode, *Scriptores rerum mythicarum latini tres Romae nuper reperti*, Celle, 1834, pp. 87 f.), but fails to repeat the somewhat more substantial account of the real Pandora as given in Fulgentius, 46, 82. In addition, he makes confusion worse confounded by appending to his fortieth chapter the explanation of the real Pandora's name according to Fulgentius, 52, 89. The "Mythographus III" repeats the Erichthonius story after "Mythographus II," 40 ("Myth. III," 10, 4; Bode, p. 223), but gives, in another place, the story of the real Pandora according to Fulgentius, 46, 82 ("Myth. III," 10, 9; Bode, pp. 227 f.).

[20] P. Abrahams, *Les Oeuvres poétiques de Baudri de Bourgueil*, Paris, 1926, p. 289 (*Carmen* CCXVI, lines 631 f.).
[21] It should be noted that an Italian humanist as erudite as Celio Calcagnino still ignores the pithos motif. In his *Super Prometheo et Epimetheo epitoma* (not included in the Basel edition of his works of 1544, but preserved, as kindly indicated to us by Professor P. O. Kristeller, in Cod. Vat. lat. 7192, fols. 204–209 v.) he merely says (fol. 206 v.): "iussit igitur [Iupiter] Vulcano [ut] effigiem puellae spetiosissimae formaret, quam deinde Pandoram nuncupatam Pallas ornauit donisque excoluit, zona scilicet, ueste argentea, ac palliolo miro artificio contexto, floribusque et aurea corona. Ab hac autem postea foemineum genus defluxit ad hominum iacturam natum, quod inter viros ita versatur ut inter apes fuci. Sine quo stare vita diutius nequeat, neque una habitare facile possit."

know more Greek than he did, Boccaccio was not satisfied with the accepted and acceptable explanation of her name as *omnium munus* ("gift to all," but in the early editions of the *Genealogia* amusingly misprinted into *omnium minus*, "devoid of everything," and therefore rendered as "manca d'ogni cosa" in the Italian translations). He proposed, as an alternative, to derive Pandora's name from "*pan,* quod est totum, et *doris,* quod est amaritudo." As a result of this strange etymology, he interprets the name of the first human being—he seems to think of Pandora as a man, or at least a hermaphrodite, and in one sentence calls her "Pandorus"—as meaning "all full of bitterness" and ends his chapter with a reference to Job.[22]

Curiously enough, the Fathers of the Church are more important for the transmission—and transformation—of the myth of Pandora than the secular writers: in an attempt to corroborate the doctrine of original sin by a classical parallel, yet to oppose Christian truth to pagan fable, they likened her to Eve, a step the full effect of which was not to be felt until the sixteenth and seventeenth centuries.[23]

---

[22] Boccaccio, *Genealogia deorum,* IV, 45 (Venice edition of 1511, fol. 35 v.):

"*De Pandora homine a Prometheo facto.* 'Pandora' dicit Fulgentius nominatum esse quem Prometheus primum ex luto confecit, quod a Fulgentio ob id dictum puto quia Pandorae significatum sit in Latino 'omnium minus' [should read *munus*], eo quod non ex noticia unius tantum rei componatur sapiens, sed ex multis, et verius ex omnibus. Posset praeterea dici Pandora a 'pan,' quod est totum, et 'doris,' quod est amaritudo, quasi Pandorus [*sic*] omni amaritudine plenus. Nil enim in praesenti vita potest homo absque amaritudine possidere; quod, utrum verum sit se unus quisque excutiat. Job autem, vir sanctus et patientiae insigne specimen, volens hoc improperare humano generi dixit: 'Homo natus de muliere brevi vivens tempore multis repletus miseriis. . . .'"

Why Boccaccio should have thought that *doris* means "bitterness" seemed inexplicable to us until we remembered the beginning of Virgil's Tenth *Eclogue.* Here the name of the Nereid Doris, often metonymically used for "the sea"

in Roman poetry, is coupled with *amara* so as to denote the "bitter," briny quality of sea water as opposed to Arethusa's spring: "Sic tibi, cum fluctus subterlabere Sicanos, / Doris *amara* suam non intermisceat undam" (lines 4 ff.).

The phrase "manca d'ogni cosa," caused by the erroneous *minus,* occurs, e.g., in the Venice edition of 1606, p. 73, and still in the Venice edition of 1644, p. 69 v., even though the "Elucidario poetico," appended to this edition, correctly says: "Pandora quasi dono di tutti overo donata da tutti" (p. 59).

[23] H. Türck, *Pandora und Eva,* Weimar, 1931, is, in spite of its title, not too informative about the origin of the parallel between Pandora and Eve, which he tends to take for granted; the same is true of the otherwise valuable article by L. Séchan, "Pandore, l'Eve grecque," *Bulletin de l'Association Guillaume Budé,* XXIII, 1929, pp. 3 ff. More pertinent information is found in an old dissertation by Christian Gottlieb Schwarz submitted at Nuremberg by N. E. Zobel: *Dissertatio inauguralis de lapsu primorum humani generis parentum a paganis adumbrato,* Altorf (Franconia), 1723. Cf. below, pp. 64 f.

In his *De corona militis,* Tertullian (who, in another place, refers to *Hesiodi Pandora* as a figure of speech denoting a perfect blend or fusion of all things and, therefore, applicable to the perfection and totality of Christ)[24] rather good-naturedly, not to say humorously, insists that Eve, and not Pandora, should be credited with the first and more reasonable use of feminine fashions and ornaments: "If there ever was a certain Pandora, whom Hesiod cites as the first woman, hers was the first head to be crowned, by the Graces, with a diadem; for she received gifts from all and was hence called 'Pandora'; to us, however, Moses—a prophetic rather than a poetic shepherd—describes the first woman, Eve, as being more conveniently encircled with leaves about the middle than with flowers about the temples. Therefore, there was no Pandora." [25] It was by the Greek Fathers that the pithos incident was stressed. Gregory of Nazianzus, after having held her up as a warning example of vanity, fraudulence, immodesty, self-seeking adulation, and prurience, and after having called her, surpassing even Hesiod, a "deadly delight" (τερπωλὴ ὀλοή), concludes by reminding the faithful of the Fall of Man: "But let us pass over the fables and listen to my words, which I shall glean for you from sacred revelation; have you not heard how the bright color of the death-dealing tree once led your first parent into fraud? He was beguiled and expelled from verdant Paradise by the deceit of the Enemy and the counsel of his wife." [26] And Origen explicitly compares the story of the forbidden pithos with that of the forbidden fruit. In the Fourth Book of *Contra Celsum* he attempts to refute his opponent, who had praised the myths of the "divine

---

[24] Tertullian, *Adversus Valentinianos,* XII (*Patrologia latina,* II, col. 562). A similar Christological interpretation of Pandora is found in Irenaeus, *Contra haereticos,* II, 22, 5 (p. 325 in W. W. Harvey's edition, Cambridge, 1857), where the analogy is extended to Pelops: "cuius caro in partes a patre divisa est, et ab omnibus diis collecta et allata et compacta, Pandoram hoc modo significavit."

[25] Tertullian, *De corona militis,* VII (*ibidem,* col. 84): "Si fuit aliqua Pandora quam primam foeminarum memorat Hesiodus, hoc primum caput coronatum est a Charitibus, cum ab omnibus muneraretur, unde Pandora. Nobis vero Moyses, propheticus, non poeticus pastor, principem foeminam Evam facilius pudenda foliis, quam tempora floribus, incinctam describit. Nulla ergo Pandora." The "Moyses, propheticus, non poeticus pastor" gracefully alludes to the fact that both Hesiod and Moses (Exodus, 3:1 ff.) received their "call" while tending sheep.

[26] Gregory of Nazianzus, *Adversus mulieris se nimis ornantes,* lines 115 ff. (*Patrologia graeca,* XXXVII, cols. 891 f.).

Hesiod" as philosophical ideas in mythological dress while ridiculing Genesis. Calling this unfair, Origen claims that the story of Adam and Eve is no less susceptible of allegorical interpretation, and no less heavily fraught with "rational meaning and secret significance," than any pagan account of the creation of man. But then he turns the tables: the story of Adam and Eve, he says, may "offend understanding" if taken literally; the story of Pandora, however, is downright funny. And by way of documentation—perhaps not without being considerably amused himself—he repeats the entire passage from the *Works and Days,* interrupting the narrative only in order to call attention to the particularly comical, "laughter-provoking," effect of the pithos story, and thus provides later philologists with a number of excellent readings.[27]

[27] Origen, *Contra Celsum,* IV (*Patrologia graeca,* XI, cols. 1086 ff.). The Hesiod lines quoted by Origen are *Works and Days,* 53–82 and 90–97.

II

The Origin of the "Box":
Erasmus of Rotterdam

SINCE the works of Hesiod were not available in Latin until 1471, and Origen's *Contra Celsum* not until 1481,[1] we cannot expect a reappearance of Pandora's pithos in either art or literature before the end of the fifteenth century. And when it did reappear, the issue was at once beclouded by that curious substitution of the word *pyxis* for pithos or dolium (as both the Latin *Opera et Dies* and the Latin *Contra Celsum* have it), which was to result in the familiar phrase "Pandora's box."

Jane Harrison—the first to notice and to stress this philological accident, the consequences of which are quite out of proportion to its apparent insignificance—inclined to fix the blame, or credit, on the excellent Lelio Gregorio Giraldi. Retelling and commenting upon the story of Pandora in his *De Deis gentium . . . syntagmata* (first published, under a slightly different title, in 1548), this erudite and usually reliable author claims in fact that Jupiter, full of resentment, had sent Pandora to Prometheus "with a box most beauti-

---

[1] Hesiod was first translated by Nicolaus Valla (Niccolò della Valle, died 1473); his translation, the only one up to 1539, was published in 1471 and reprinted about twenty-five times in the following half century. Origen's *Contra Celsum* was first translated by Cristoforo Persona, whose work was published in 1481 and also frequently reprinted; see P. Koetschau's Introduction to *Origenes*, I (*Die griechischen christlichen Schriftsteller der ersten drei Jahrhunderte*), Berlin, 1899, p. lxxiv.

ful but concealing within every kind of calamity" ("cum pyxide pulcherrima illa quidem, sed intus omne calamitatis genus abscondente").[2]

Miss Harrison's hypothesis, though not proposed without judicious reservations, has crystallized into a dogma in all recent literature, amplified only by the suggestion that Giraldi may have been misled by classical reliefs, vases, or cameos showing a female figure with a little vase or jewel box.[3] We shall see, however, that at least one pictorial representation of Pandora with a box (*fig. 16*) more than probably antedates the writing, and certainly antedates the publication, of Giraldi's *Syntagmata*; and even without this external evidence it would be intrinsically improbable that the statement of a learned mythographer, an admirable scholar but known only to an intellectual elite, should have sufficed to bring about the international acceptance of a new image and a new locution.

The person really responsible for "Pandora's box" (and honest Giraldi more than hints at this)[4] is none other than Erasmus of Rotterdam, and the pulpit from which he preached his heresy was his *Adagiorum chiliades tres* (first edition, 1508), one of the world's most popular and influential books. Here the story of Pandora and her pithos occurs not once but twice; and in both cases the pithos is transformed into a pyxis that is supposed to have been brought to earth by Pandora.

By way of exemplifying the proverb *Hostium munera non munera* ("the gifts of enemies are not gifts"), Erasmus says: "Ita ut fuit pyxis illa fallax, per Pandoram a Iove Prometheo missa."[5] And in illustration of the proverb

---

[2] L. G. Gyraldus (Giraldi), *De Deis gentium varia et multipla historia, in qua simul de eorum imaginibus et cognominibus agitur*, Basel (Oporinus), 1548. The second edition, often erroneously referred to as the first, was published by the same publisher in 1560 and is entitled *De Deis gentium varia et multipla historia, libris sive syntagmatibus* XVII *comprehensa*. We quote from *Opera omnia*, Leiden, 1696, I, pp. 415 f.

[3] Pauly-Wissowa, *op. cit.*, col. 538.

[4] Giraldi's summary of Hesiod's account concludes as follows: "Ad quam rem scriptores alludunt et Erasmus in proverbio perstringit *Malo accepto stultus sapit.*"

[5] Erasmus of Rotterdam, *Adagiorum chiliades tres*, I, ccxxxiii. In the *editio princeps*, Venice, 1508 (Aldus), fol. 35 v. (with ccxxxiii misprinted into cccxxxiii); in the Basel edition of 1520 (Froben), p. 98. The phrase ἄδωρα δῶρα, alluded to in the proverb *Hostium munera non munera* and actually quoted in Erasmus' commentary on the proverb *Malo accepto*, comes from Sophocles' *Aias*, line 650. In the precursor of Erasmus' *Adagia*, the *Adagiorum collectanea* (first edition, Paris, 1500), Pandora is not as yet mentioned.

Malo accepto stultus sapit ("the fool gets wise after having been hurt"),
he gives the entire passage that, with only one negligible verbal change, was
to reappear in Giraldi's *Syntagmata:* "Iupiter iratus Prometheo propter
ignem furtum, sublatum e coelo ac mortalibus redditum, cupiensque illum
simili retaliare dolo, Vulcano negocium dat, ut e luto puellae simulachrum
quanto posset artificio fingat. Id simul atque factum est, singulos deos
deasque monet, ut ei simulachro suas quisque dotes adiungerent. Unde et
virgini Pandorae nomen affictum apparet. Hanc igitur omnibus formae,
cultus, ingenii, linguaeque dotibus cumulatam, Iupiter cum pyxide pulcherrima quidem illa, sed intus omne calamitatum genus occulente, ad Prometheum mittit. Is recusato munere, fratrem admonet, ut siquid muneris sese
absente mitteretur, ne reciperet. Redit Pandora, persuasoque Epimetheo
pyxidem donat. Eam simul ac aperuisset, evolantibusque morbis, sensisset
Iovis ἄδωρα δῶρα, sero nimirum sapere coepit." [6] "Jupiter, angry at Prometheus because of the stolen fire he had abstracted from heaven and handed
over to the mortals, and wishing to take his revenge by a similar fraud, com-
manded Vulcan to form out of clay, as skillfully as he could, the image of a
maiden. This done, he asked all the gods and goddesses each to bestow a
gift upon this image; hence, it appears, the maiden was named Pandora. This
maiden, then, showered with all the gifts of beauty, grooming, intelligence,
and eloquence, was sent to Prometheus with a box, it, too, most beautiful in
shape but concealing within every kind of calamity. Prometheus refused this
present and admonished his brother not to accept any present delivered
in his absence. Pandora returns, captivating Epimetheus and presenting the
box to him. As soon as he [or she] had opened it, so that the evils flew out,
and as soon as he had realized that Jupiter's gifts were 'no-gifts,' he surely
became a wise man too late."

---

[6] Erasmus, *Adagiorum chiliades tres*, I, xxxi.
In the *editio princeps*, fol. 12r. / v.; in the
Basel edition of 1520, pp. 31 f. It is interesting
to note that as late and humanistically minded
an author as Achille Bocchi, *Symbolicae* *Quaestiones*, Bologna, 1555, III, 67, p. cxlii,
illustrates the proverb *Malo accepto* in good
medieval (that is to say, Biblical) fashion by
the fool's being flogged ("a rod for the fool's
back," "Tousjours au fol la masse").

This Latin summary of the Pandora story in its entirety—so far as we know, the first ever attempted—established what may be called the "modern," as opposed to all classical, versions. The replacement of πίθος or *dolium* by *pyxis* transformed a big, practically immovable storage jar into a small, portable vessel; and the precise and reiterated assertion that Jupiter "sent" this vessel to Prometheus by Pandora (*"pyxis* illa fallax, *per Pandoram* a Iove Prometheo *missa," "Hanc* . . . Iupiter *cum pyxide* pulcherrima . . . ad Prometheum *mittit"*) explicitly ascribes to her the function of transporting it to earth. Moreover, Erasmus' narrative could seem to imply, by virtue of a grammatical ambiguity, which has been indicated in our translation, that it was Epimetheus rather than Pandora who committed the actual offense.

Rejected by Prometheus, Erasmus tells us, Pandora turns to his brother, who accepts her, and gives him the pyxis. But in the following sentence, beginning with "Eam simul" and ending with "sapere coepit," *Epimetheus* remains, from a strictly grammatical point of view, the subject of the clause "Eam simul ac aperuisset" (even though the *aperuisset* is probably intended to refer back to *Pandora*). Thus it appears to be he who opens the "box," and this seeming endorsement of an obscure and freakish variant of the Pandora story, for which there is no other authority than Philodemus of Gadara,[7] accounts, we believe, for the otherwise inexplicable fact that several poets and artists from the sixteenth to the nineteenth century depict Epimetheus opening Pandora's box.[8]

Why did Erasmus, who certainly knew his languages and in his own edition of Origen's works was careful to preserve the correct rendering of πίθος as *dolium*,[9] transform the image of a woman yielding to the temptation of an enormous storage jar into the image of a woman carrying with her a small and handsome pyxis? He might, of course, have seen and misinterpreted some picture of the Magdalene with her ointment jar or one of those

[7] See above, p. 8.   [8] See below, pp. 79 ff.
[9] *Originis Adamantis . . . opera, per Des[iderium].
Erasmum Roterodamum,* Basel (Froben), 1536, p. 642.

antique representations of young women with a little vase or jewel box; but it is far more probable that he, his philological instinct sensing a connection evident even to an educated painter of the eighteenth century,[10] fused—or confused—the crucial episode in the life of Hesiod's Pandora with its near duplicate in Roman literature, the last and equally crucial episode in the life of Apuleius' Psyche.

Having acquitted herself of three other seemingly impossible tasks imposed upon her by Venus, Psyche is finally handed a pyxis, which she has to carry down to Hades and to bring back, filled with "a little bit [*modicum*] of Persephone's beauty." [11] Psyche succeeds, against all odds, in being admitted to the presence of Persephone, from whom she "receives the pyxis filled and sealed" ("repletam conclusamque pyxidem suscipit"). But on her way back —and this is a motif obviously borrowed from the myth of Pandora—she cannot resist the temptation of opening it. Overcome by the vapors released from the pyxis, she faints and is rescued only by the personal intervention of Cupid, who revives her, reseals the beauty-bearing vessel ("reserat pyxidem"), and thus enables her to accomplish her mission.

It was, we think, with this description in mind that Erasmus remodeled Pandora in the image of Psyche. Even in contrasting the handsome appearance of her vessel—a point not stressed in any previous source—with the sinister nature of its contents, he seems to have been influenced by another reminiscence from Apuleius: just before being dispatched to Persephone with her pyxis, Psyche had been ordered to fetch a sample of the ill-boding Stygian waters in a "little urn" (*urnula*), which is described as "a small vase carved of crystal" ("crystallo dedolatum vasculum").[12]

Be that as it may, in nearly all European languages the phrases "Pandora's box," "boîte de Pandore," "caja de Pandora," "Pandoras ask," "doos van Pandora," "Büchse der Pandora," came to be accepted as idiomatic, denoting any source of multiple disaster from original sin to an undesirable

---

[10] See below, p. 89.   [11] Apuleius, *Metamorphoses*, VI, 16, 20, 21.
[12] *Ibidem*, VI, 13, 38.

piece of municipal legislation, and furnishing the titles for many a play or novel centered around an attractive but destructive specimen of femininity.[13] The only exception is, characteristically, Italy, less deeply committed to Erasmus than the transalpine world. Here the vernacular adhered, and adheres to this day, to *"vaso* di Pandora,"[14] and only the Latin-writing humanists—unless they were conscientious or pedantic enough to retain the orthodox *dolium*—inclined to yield to the Erasmian fashion, at least to the extent of reducing the size of the vessel to that of a "vasculum."[15]

Needless to say, this substitution of Psyche's pyxis, urnula, or vasculum for Pandora's pithos or dolium—occasionally complicated by the old

[13] For early English occurrences of the phrase "Pandora's box" we must refer the reader to the listings in Bartlett's *Familiar Quotations*, B. Stevenson, *The Home Book of Quotations*, and *The Oxford English Dictionary*, which adduces, as the earliest instance, a passage in Stephen Gossen's *School of Abuse* of 1579. We limit ourselves to quoting a passage of Ben Jonson: "Pox on thee, Vulcan, thy Pandora's pox, / And all the Evils that flew out of her box / Light on thee" (*The Execution of Vulcan*, in *Epigrams*, F. Underwood, ed., New York, 1936, pp. 213 f.). It should be noted, though, that Jonson—in a very special context and with even broader humor—speaks of Pandora's vessel as a "tub": "Such was Pythagoras' thigh, Pandora's tub" (*The Alchemist*, II, 1, 92). In their commentary (*Ben Jonson*, x, Oxford, 1950, p. 72), C. H. Herford and P. Simpson correctly derive the whole passage—a jocular enumeration of objects supposedly connected with alchemy, beginning with a wooden book written by Adam in "high-Dutch"—from a passage in Martin Delrio's *Disquisitiones magicae* (see below, n. 4, p. 69), where, however, Pandora's vessel is designated as *poculum*. The allusion to "Pythagoras' thigh," also borrowed from Delrio, refers to an old story, already ridiculed in Lucian's *Verae Historiae*, II, 21, according to which Pythagoras had a thigh of pure gold (see, e.g., Diogenes Laërtius, *De vitis . . . clarorum philosophorum*, VIII, 1, 9)—a story that, like the Pandora myth, was believed to have alchemistic significance. As to book titles, suffice it to mention Frank Wedekind's rather remarkable *Die Büchse der Pandora* (English

translation, entitled *Pandora's Box*, New York, 1918), J. A. Mitchell's less remarkable *Pandora's Box*, New York, 1911, and, as the most recent instance, H. Edinga, *Adieu, Pandora!*, The Hague, 1954.

[14] As a particularly amusing example we may quote a passage from Galileo's youthful diatribe against academic (and other) habiliments, the *Capitulo contra il portar la toga*, lines 91 ff.:

*E s'una donna avea qualche magagna,
La teneva coperta solamente
Con tre o quattro foglie di castagna;
Così non era gabbata la gente,
Come si vede che l'è gabbat'ora,
Se già l'uomo non è più ch'intendente:
Chè tal per buona, veduta di fuora,
Che se tu la ricerchi sotto panno,
La trovi come'l vaso di Pandora.
E così d'ogni frode e d'ogn'inganno
Si vede chiaro che n'è sol cagione
L'andar vestito tutto quanto l'anno.*

(Galileo Galilei, *Scritti letterari*, A. Chiari, ed., Florence, 1943, pp. 5 f.)

[15] Natalis Comes (Natale Conti), *Mythologiae* . . . , IV, 6 (first published in 1551, here quoted from the Frankfurt edition of 1596), p. 316, uses *vasculum* twice and *vas* only once. The anonymous *Eruditissimi viri Hieroglyphicorum commentariorum liber* appended to the later editions of Pierio Valeriano's *Hieroglyphica* (first published in 1556) has *vasculum* once and *pyxis* twice; see, e.g., the Lyons edition of 1611, p. 632, or the Frankfurt edition of 1678, p. 745.

but erroneous identification of Pandora with Pandrosus [16]—resulted in considerable confusion in Renaissance art as well as in modern scholarship. Since both Psyche and Pandora had come to be equipped with small recepta-

1. ADRIAEN DE VRIES: *Psyche Carried to Heaven*

[16] See above, p. 9. A drawing by Salomon de Bray, dated 1663, in the Fodor Museum at Amsterdam (J. W. von Moltke, "Salomon de Bray," *Marburger Jahrbuch für Kunstwissenschaft,* XI / XII, 1938–1939, p. 352, fig. 41), described as "Erichthonius wird von Pandora befreit," certainly represents the opening of Erichthonius' basket by Pandrosus and her sisters, and the same would seem to be true of a picture by Rubens that is described as a "korfken van Bandora [*sic*]" in the correspondence of the art dealer Forchoudt (J. Denucé, *Exportation d'oeuvres d'art au 17ᵉ siècle à Anvers,* The Hague, 1931, p. 259). This interpretation of the reference, which was brought to our attention by Professor Julius S. Held, is all the more probable as two original pictures by Rubens representing the discovery of Erichthonius are still in existence, one in the Liechtenstein Gallery at Vienna, the other in the Museum at Oberlin College, Oberlin, Ohio (cf. L. Burchard, "Rubens' Daughters of Cecrops," *Allen Memorial Museum Bulletin,* XI, 1953, pp. 4 ff.).

cles, now shaped like a box in the proper sense of the word, now like a larg-
ish pomander, now like a little vase (as in Raphael's famous fresco in the
Villa Farnesina and its derivatives, among them a beautiful bronze group
by Adriaen de Vries, *fig. 1*),[17] now like a goblet,[18] it is not always easy to decide

2. FOLLOWER OF MARCANTONIO RAIMONDI:
Psyche (?) Brought to Earth by Mercury

3. FOLLOWER OF MARCANTONIO RAIMONDI:
Psyche (?) Carried to Heaven by Mercury

which of the two, or even whether either of the two, is meant. Two engravings
from the school of Marcantonio listed as *Pandora Brought to Earth by Mercury* and *Pandora Carried Back to Heaven by Mercury* (*figs. 2* and *3*) leave

[17] Stockholm, Nationalmuseum, apparently
based upon the engraving B. XIV, No. 5, rather
than upon Raphael's fresco. For literature, see
De Triomf van het Maniërisme (catalogue of
an exhibition held at the Rijksmuseum in Amsterdam, July 1–October 16, 1955), p. 183, No.
379, where the group is absurdly entitled
"Psyche met de doos van Pandora."
[18] For a text explicitly speaking of "Pandorae poculum," see n. 4, p. 69.

the beholder in doubt as to whether the artist had Psyche or Pandora in mind; but all the odds are in favor of the first alternative.[19] The central fig-

4. BARTOLOMMEO MELIOLI:
Personification of Health

[19] Bartsch, xv, p. 35, Nos. 1 and 2. The difficulty is that the iconographical data (a nude woman transported through the air by Mercury, descending in one print and rising in the other, but carrying a vase on both trips) do not agree with either myth. Psyche commutes, as it were, between the heavens and the lower spheres, but is accompanied by Mercury only on the occasion of her final apotheosis (Apuleius, vi, 23), when she no longer carries any vessel. Pandora, on the other hand, is conveyed to earth by Mercury, but never returns to heaven at all; even if we were to imagine that she does so, she could not possibly have taken along that fatal "box" which, with all its contents save Hope evaporated, constitutes her legacy to mankind. Given the fact that the artist belonged to a circle close to Raphael, we may assume that his two engravings represent an understandable, if somewhat confused, variation on motifs suggested by the immensely popular Farnesina cycle (Psyche carrying a vase, though borne by three *putti* and not by Mercury, and Psyche borne by Mercury, though not carrying a vase) rather than an original but quite preposterous redaction of the then fairly little-known Pandora story. Psyche rather than Pandora would also seem to have been the subject of a lost bronze group by Giovanni da Bologna, described as *L'Enlèvement* (!) *de Pandore par Mercure*, which was in the gardens of the Château de Marly after having passed through the hands of Queen Christina of Sweden and Colbert (Piganiol de la Force, *Nouvelle Description des Châteaux et Parcs de Versailles et de Marly*, ninth ed., Paris, 1764, ii, p. 292, referred to in Larousse, *Grand Dictionnaire universel*, xii, p. 111, *s.v.* "Pandore").

ure on the reverse of Bartolommeo Melioli's medal on the recovery of Francesco II Gonzaga (*fig. 4*) is not Pandora, but a personification of Health (cf. *figs.* 5 and 6), who, surrounded by symbols of the elements, holds in her

5. Healthful Nature and Madness
Ferrarese bronze

6. The Natural Philosopher Amidst the Elements
Ferrarese bronze

hands two ears of corn (indicative of wholesome nourishment) and a small basket filled with medicines and therefore inscribed with the word *cautius* (*scil., sumantur* or *componantur*).[20] A ceiling decoration executed in 1745

[20] F. Hill, *A Corpus of Italian Medals of the Renaissance before Cellini*, London, 1930, p. 48, No. 196, Plate 36. The reverse of the medal is inscribed ADOLESCENTIAE AVGVSTAE, while the inscription of the obverse reads: D. FRANCISCVS. GON[zaga]. D. FRED[erici]. III. M[archio]. MANTVAE. F[ilius]. SPES. PUB[lica]. SALVSQV. P[ublica]. REDIVI [va]. It has long been assumed that the medal was struck after Francesco's recovery from a dangerous illness in 1484. Hill, on the contrary, believes that it must date before the death of Francesco's father, Federigo, on July 14, 1481: the phrase *Franciscus Frederici filius*, he thinks, characterizes Francesco as a crown prince. It would seem, however, that a reference to a young ruler's distinguished father would be permissible even after his own accession to the throne; in fact, it would have

been rather unflattering to Federigo if, during his lifetime, his son had been greeted as "the revived hope and welfare of the commonwealth." Be that as it may, the word *rediviva* appears more suitable for the commemoration of a recovery from illness than for any other occasion, and this interpretation is borne out by the fact that the attributes of the personification on the reverse recur, in part, in an unequivocally medical context: on a sumptuously decorated bronze mortar, now in the National Gallery at Washington, which is also of north Italian origin. This mortar—adorned with the Este coat of arms impaled with the French, and therefore probably dating from the reign of Ercole II (1535–1559), husband of Renée of France—may have been executed for the medical faculty of the Studio Ferrarese, then especially famed for medical studies, as a gift of

by Jacob de Wit—the "Rubens of the eighteenth century"—and transmitted to us through the preparatory drawing in the Teyler Museum at Haarlem (*fig. 7*) does not show, as stated in the catalogue, "Pandora Dispatched to

7. JACOB DE WIT: *Apotheosis of Psyche*

Earth by Jupiter" but the *Apotheosis of Psyche* according to Apuleius, VI, 23.[21] And a drawing by C. A. Teunissen in the Ashmolean Museum at Oxford

---

the Duke or for the Duke as a gift of the medical faculty. In accordance with its purpose, the compounding of medicines, its body is decorated with four allegories glorifying the healing profession. First, Death and Time, the forces to be held at bay by the physician. Second, Two Eagles Fighting a Snake, a symbol of the conquest of evil in general and disease in particular (cf. R. Wittkower, "Eagle and Serpent," *Journal of the Warburg and Courtauld Institutes*, II, 1939, pp. 293 ff., especially pp. 308, 310 f.) and, at the same time, an allusion to the heraldic eagle of the Este family; according to Cesare Ripa's *Iconologia* the eagle stands, among other things, for "Salubrità" and "Purità dell'Aria." Third (*fig. 5*), a personification of the beneficial, health-giving forces of nature, viz., a nude woman placing her fingers on the nipples of her abundant breasts (see Ripa, *s.v.* "Benignità," "Natura," "Sostanza"), confronted with a seated man who, by trying to break a heavy and enormously involved chain, signifies raving madness (see Ripa, *s.v.* "Furore" and "Furore implaca-

(*fig. 8*), officially described as *Pandora and the Fettered Prometheus*, represents in reality the very incident that, we believe, gave rise to the whole

8. C. A. TEUNISSEN: *Psyche Before Persephone*

---

bile"). And, fourth (*fig. 6*), the Perfect Physician or Natural Philosopher (for his compass,
see, e.g., Ripa, *s.v.* "Consideratione" or "Opera-
tione perfetta"), seated in a pose of deep re-
flection and surrounded by the Four Elements
(which correspond to the four humors, the
four seasons, the four directions of space, etc.),
the equilibrium of which means health while
their imbalance means disease. In Melioli's
medal only Fire and Water are indicated by
separate symbols, but the element Earth can be
taken to be expressed by the piece of terrain
on which the familiar figure stands, and that of
Air by the ambient space. Hill's assumption

that the two symbols of Water and Fire represent the "dangers in the path of youth" cannot be supported by evidence.
[21] H. J. Scholten, *Musée Teyler à Haarlem,
Catalogue raisonné des dessins des écoles
française et hollandaise,* Haarlem, 1904, p.
369. The drawing—a sketch for a painted ceiling, brought to our attention by Professor J. G.
van Gelder, who also kindly provided the
photograph reproduced in *fig. 7*—is preserved
in Portefeuille T, No. 61. That it represents
the apotheosis of Psyche is evident, first, from
the absence of any *boîte*; second, from the fact
that the heroine is obviously transported not

confusion: in the foreground Psyche is shown receiving the pyxis from Persephone (the latter uniquely determined by her snake and a great number of attending demons), and in the background she opens it while Cupid, prepared for the inevitable emergency, looks on from a mountaintop.[22]

---

to earth but heavenward, which never happened to Pandora (see n. 19, p. 22). According to a remark added by the painter himself, the ceiling decoration prepared by the drawing was executed in 1745 for a gentleman named Willem Kops Nicolaasz, residing at Haarlem.

[22] K. T. Parker, *Catalogue of the Collection of Drawings in the Ashmolean Museum*, Oxford, 1938, p. 33, No. 79. We are grateful to Mr. Parker for kindly having supplied us with a photograph.

Of some Renaissance portrayals of young women holding a box or vessel it is hard to say whether they are meant to represent Psyche, Hygea, Artemisia, or Mary Magdalene; but none of them is unequivocally characterized as Pandora. We mention an allegedly French painting of *c.* 1510 (to judge from the reproduction, of very questionable authenticity) illustrated in *Auktionskatalog F. Helbing*, Frankfurt, May 3, 1932; a pen drawing by J. Muller, dated 1627, in J. de Kempenaer's *Album amicorum* (in 1925 in the possession of Mmes de Kempenaer, Haarlem, and shown at the Grotius Tentoonstelling, The Hague, 1925, No. 1107); and a picture in a private collection at Paris, ascribed to Jean Cousin, illustrated in H. de Hevesy, "L'Histoire véridique de la Joconda," *Gazette des*

Beaux-Arts, ser. 6, XL, 1952, pp. 4 ff., fig. 19, for which see below, p. 87, note. An early sixteenth-century wood statue in the Musée de Cluny at Paris, ascribed to the French school and christened *Pandore* in the earlier catalogues (and so referred to in Larousse, *loc. cit.*), has been attributed to the Flemish school and rechristened *Sainte Madeleine* in 1925 (Musée de Cluny, *Catalogue des bois sculptées et meubles*, Haraucourt, ed., No. 63). Piero di Cosimo's Prometheus *Cassone* at Strasbourg (P. Schubring, *Cassoni*, Leipzig, 1915, Plate XCVI, No. 14; cf. K. Habich, "Ueber zwei Prometheus-Bilder angeblich von Piero di Cosimo," *Sitzungsberichte der bayrischen Akademie der Wissenschaften, phil.-hist. Klasse*, 1920, No. 2, and K. Borinski, "Die Deutung der Piero di Cosimo zugeschriebenen Prometheus-Bilder," *ibidem*, No. 12) does not include, assertions to the contrary notwithstanding, the figure of Pandora at all. Her animation by Prometheus is, however, represented in an unattractive seventeenth-century painting, presumably French, where she is shown seated on a block of marble while Prometheus applies the life-giving torch to her breast (*Verzeichnis der Gemälde, Gypse und Bronzen in der Grossherzoglichen Sammlung zu Oldenburg*, 1881, No. 291).

III

Pandora and Hope:
Andrea Alciati

How, then, did the real Pandora, as opposed to all these pseudo-Pandoras, make her appearance in Renaissance art? Significantly, not in Italy, but in the North; and, even more significantly, in two different ways. Where art was subservient to erudition, the development began with the exploitation of Pandora's authentic attribute, the pithos or dolium, detached from her person; where art, though benefiting by erudition, retained its independence, the development began with a revival of Pandora's person designated by her nonauthentic attribute, the pyxis.

The first of these two processes took place in the woodcut illustrations of Andrea Alciati's *Emblemata*, parent to an innumerable progeny of other emblem books, which contains two interrelated emblems concerned with the idea of hope. In one, entitled *In simulacrum Spei*, Hope is described as carrying the broken weapons of death and accompanied by Cupid and *Bonus Eventus*, while Nemesis stands near in order to warn that hope should not be directed toward that which is forbidden: "Scilicet ut speres nil nisi quod liceat." [1] The other, entitled *Illicitum non sperandum*, merely re-emphasizes this warning by showing Hope and Nemesis in direct juxtaposition; in fact,

---

[1] This passage explains the fact that the statue of Hope on a seventeenth-century confessional in the Béguinage at Malines (Phot. ACL 78271B) holds a palm branch in one hand and the bridle of Nemesis in the other.

*9. Hope, Nemesis, Bonus Eventus,
and Love*
From Alciati, *Emblemata*

the accompanying distich simply appends the pentameter just quoted (except for the fact that a *non* is substituted for the *nil*) to the hexameter "Spes simul et Nemesis nostris altaribus adsunt."

In the first illustrated edition of Alciati's work, published by Steyner at Augsburg in 1531, the same crude little woodcut was used for both these emblems. It shows Nemesis, with sword and bridle, standing on the left; Hope, holding a broken spear, standing on the right; and Cupid and *Bonus Eventus* sitting on the ground between them (*fig. 9*).[2] For the second edition, published by Wechel at Augsburg in 1534, however, two separate and more sophisticated illustrations were devised. And in these new woodcuts—reused in the third edition, published by Wechel at Paris in 1536, and repeated, with minor variations, in countless later ones—the faithful illustration of five hitherto neglected lines in the long poem that describes the *Simulacrum Spei* gave rise to an entirely different and novel iconography:

"Why do you [Hope is asked] *lazily sit on the cover of a vat* [dolium]?"
"Because [she answers] *I alone stayed at home while all the evils fluttered
    about everywhere,
  As the hallowed Muse of the Ascraean sage has told us."*
*"Which bird is accompanying you?" "The crow, most faithful of augurs;
  When he cannot say, 'All is well,' he says, 'All will be well.' "*[3]

[2] Andrea Alciati, *Emblemata*, Augsburg (Steyner), 1531, fols. A6 v. and D8 v.

[3] Alciati, *Emblemata*, Augsburg (Wechel), 1534, pp. 82 f.; *ibidem*, Paris (Wechel), 1536, fols. L4 v.–L6 r. In the 1531 edition, where the same wood block had to serve for both the *In simulacrum Spei* and the *Illicitum non sperandum*, these two emblems had to be printed on separate signatures. From 1534 on, when two separate blocks were available, they could follow each other immediately. In the later editions, where the emblems are numbered consecutively, the *In simulacrum Spei* emblem appears as No. XLIIII, the *Illicitum non sperandum* emblem as No. XLVI. The text of the former reads as follows:

Even without the excellent commentary by Claude Mignot (Claudius
Minos), appended to most Alciati editions after 1571, no one could fail
to see that the quotation from the
"Ascraean sage" refers to Hesiod's
tale of Pandora and her pithos; and
the additional references to the crow
—who always holds out a promise
by saying "Cras, cras," "Tomorrow,
tomorrow" [4]—strangely yet lastingly
connected this harsh-voiced bird with
Hope, on the one hand, and Pandora,
on the other.

10. Hope and Nemesis
From Alciati, *Emblemata*

The woodcut of the *Illicitum non
sperandum* emblem (*fig. 10*) [5] is ob-

---

*Quae Dea tam laeto suspectans sidera vultu?
Cuius peniculis reddita imago fuit?
Elpidii fecere manus. Ego nominor illa,
Quae miseris promptam Spes bona praestat
opem.
Cur viridis tibi palla? Quod omnia me duce
vernent.
Quid manibus mortis tela refracta geris?
Quod vivos sperare decet, praecido sepultis.
Cur in dolioli tegmine pigra sedes?
Sola domi mansi volitantibus undique noxis,
Ascraei ut docuit musa verenda senis.
Quae tibi adest volucris? Cornix fidissimus
oscen;
Est bene cum nequeat dicere, dicit, Erit.*

[4] Claudius Minos correctly remarks in his
Commentary that the last line of the foregoing
poem is adapted from a distich quoted in Sue-
tonius' *Life of Domitian* (XXIII, 2) :

*Nuper Tarpeio qui sedit culmine cornix
"Est bene" non potuit dicere, dixit: "Erit."*

Alciati's second and no less important source

is, however, Tibullus, *Carmina*, II, 6, 20:

*. . . credula vitam
Spes fovet et melius cras fore semper erit.*

It may be noted that pre-Alciatian iconography tended to invest the talking crow with
a less favorable significance. As kindly brought
to our attention by Mr. Frederick B. Adams,
Jr., Geoffroy Tory's Books of Hours (Paris,
1525 and 1531, here fol. P VIII r.) contain a
woodcut where a crow saying "cras, cras" is
perched on a bare tree while winged Death,
armed with spear and hourglass, triumphantly
proceeds over a heap of prostrate victims. And
in illustrating the thirty-first chapter of Sebastian Brant's *Narrenschyff*, Basel, 1494, entitled "Von Aufschub suchen," Dürer represented the fool given to procrastination accompanied by no less than three crows saying
"crasz."
[5] Alciati, *Emblemata*, Augsburg (Wechel),
1534, p. 84; *ibidem*, Paris (Wechel), 1536,
fols. L6 v.–L7 4.; in later editions, Emblem
XLVI.

viously adapted from a late-medieval type where the figure of Hope is almost suffocated by attributes: regally enthroned, she has a ship on her head, a sickle and a beehive in her hands, and a bird cage at her feet (*fig. 11*).[6] The

11. Hope
Stained-glass window (1519)

rather pedestrian woodcut designer replaced the throne with a drumlike barrel[7] and the sickle with the broken weapons of death. He omitted the

[6] This type seems first to occur in Rouen, Bibliothèque Municipale, ms. 927, fol. 17 v., where, however, the Virtues are represented standing. For this manuscript, see E. Mâle, *L'Art religieux de la fin du Moyen Age en France*, 3rd ed., Paris, 1925, pp. 311 ff.; E. van Moë, "Les *Ethiques, Poétiques* et *Economiques* d'Aristote," *Les Trésors des Bibliothèques de France*, III, fascicule IX, 1930, pp. 3 ff., Plate I, 1 (with tentative explanation of the caged bird as a symbol of hope for freedom). The stained-glass window reproduced in our *fig. 11* represents an intermediary between this type and the Alciati woodcut in that the figure is shown enthroned.

[7] In later Alciati editions, the *Illicitum non sperandum* woodcut was replaced by a more realistic one in which the drumlike barrel assumed the appearance of a wooden cask as seen in the *Simulacrum Spei* picture.

ship and the beehive. But he retained the bird cage as a convenient means of introducing the crow. In illustrating the *Simulacrum Spei,* on the other

12. *Hope, Bonus Eventus, and Love*
From Alciati, *Emblemata*

hand, a more skillful designer, bidding good-by to the late-medieval tradition, proceeded exclusively on the basis of Alciati's poem and the original Hesiod text. In his woodcut (*fig. 12*) the dolium is realistically rendered as a vat or cask composed of wooden staves, and the feet of the crow—who says "Cras, cras" with all his might—are caught beneath the cover of this cask just as, in Hesiod's *Work and Days,* Hope had been "stopped by the lid of the jar."

Owing to the enormous influence of Alciati's *Emblemata,* the crow became a widely accepted, though often imperfectly understood, symbol of Hope in humanistic iconography, particularly in the Netherlands. It can be encountered in engravings by such masters as Maarten van Heemskerck, Cornelis Floris, and Hendrik Goltzius (*figs. 13* and *14*),[8] and it became

[8] In Maarten van Heemskerck's *Speculum diversarum imaginum speculativarum* (*Temporis vires et diversitas*) the horses drawing the triumphal chariot of Humility are led by a Spes holding an anchor in her right hand while a crow is perched on her left (*fig. 13*). A figure similarly equipped serves as a caryatid in the *Tomb of a Knight,* an influential engraving by Cornelis Floris (*fig. 14*); and a majestic bird, obviously intended to be but not looking very much like a crow, is perched on a wooden obelisk in Hendrik Goltzius' engraving *Spes.* Here, as in other cases, the artist was apparently not clear in his mind as to the precise ornithological nature of a bird known to him only through representational tradition.

13. MAARTEN VAN HEEMSKERCK: *Triumph of Humility*

14. CORNELIS FLORIS: *Tomb of a Knight*

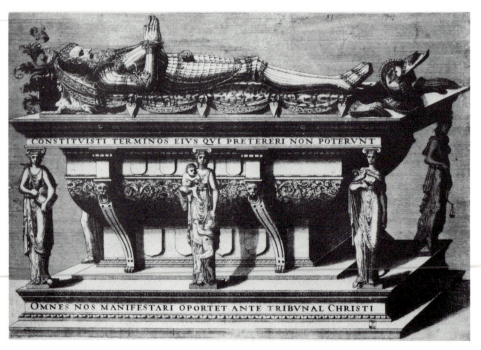

a real vogue in Flemish sculpture (*fig. 15*), where more than half a dozen instances have come to our notice.[9] On the other hand, however, it became,

for a time, an attribute of Pandora. Where Hope was thought of as a human figure, the bold Hesiodian image of her "being stopped by the lid," "remaining in the unbreakable home," or even "staying under the rim of the vessel" could be visualized only by some sort of trickery: the figure had to be reduced in size and either shown within the vessel as in transparency (*fig. 49*) or represented on its outer surface as a kind of relief or niello (*fig. 57*). The little bird, however, was easily manageable. And it was the first major artist to bring Pandora on the stage in person, and to show her in action, who availed himself of the opportunity of introducing Hope in the guise of a crow: Rosso Fiorentino.

15. JÉRÔME DUQUES-NOY THE ELDER: *Hope*

[9] The following cases may be quoted: Jérôme Duquesnoy the Elder, caryatid from the tabernacle in the Collégiale St.-Martin at Aalst (Phot. ACL 37272B, our *fig. 15*), apparently derived from the above-mentioned *Tomb of a Knight* by Cornelis Floris; caryatid supporting the pulpit in St. James's at Bruges, dated 1694 (Phot. ACL 128445B); caryatid on a confessional in St. Michael's at Louvain (Phot. ACL 72661A); caryatid supporting the tabernacle in St. Peter's at Turnhout (Phot. ACL 27951B); caryatid on a cupboard owned by Baroness Lunden at Humbeck Castle (Phot. ACL 88150B). In an eighteenth-century relief, surmounting the door of a house at Bruges, Markt No. 28, Hope is shown reclining but still equipped with an anchor and an enormous crow (Phot. ACL 67690A). In the choir stalls of St. Amandus' at Geel, dated 1693, the crow has been replaced with a falcon (Phot. ACL 36222B).

IV

Pandora and Ignorance:
Rosso Fiorentino

N AN admirable pen drawing, preserved in the École des Beaux-Arts at Paris (*fig. 16*),[1] Rosso goes straight to the heart of the matter: he shows the crucial scene, the opening of the vessel; and his interpretation of this scene is not only the earliest but the only one to do justice to its terrifying possibilities. In contrast to all his followers, he realized that diminutive demons escaping from a small receptacle and swarming about like so many mosquitoes are apt to strike the beholder as a nuisance rather than a tragedy; he had the courage to represent the Vices as full-scale human figures.

Pandora, her beautiful body only half concealed by a billowing drapery, has lifted the lid off a round, flat, metal box—the Erasmian pyxis, here making its first appearance in art. From its rim there hangs—"stopped," not so much by the lid as by a kind of magnetic attraction emanating from the vessel itself—the now-familiar crow.[2] But Pandora's action results, not in the release of figures small enough to have been confined to the box, but in a terrific explosion. Out of a blinding flash of light and power there emerges, gestures and attitudes still dominated by the centrifugal forces that have set them free,

---

[1] K. Kusenberg, *Le Rosso*, Paris, 1931, p. 144, Plate LXXVII; P. Barocchi, *Il Rosso Fiorentino*, Rome, 1950, pp. 108, 128, 131, 173 f., 214 f., fig. 192.
[2] Barocchi, *op. cit.*, p. 215, mistakes the crow for the dove of peace, "appesa al orlo dell' antica prigione," and interprets this motif as expressing the same "ironia che sprizza delle mani e del naso impertinente di Pomona."

16. ROSSO FIORENTINO: *Pandora Opening the Box*

a cluster of life-sized human figures conceived, as in Michelangelo's *Dream*, not as the troubles and diseases of the pagan myth, but as the Seven Deadly Sins of Christian theology. We recognize, reading from left to right, Sloth, supported by a stick, and, behind her, a huddled and contorted figure, which may or may not stand for Luxury; Pride, reaching for heaven with arms outstretched; Wrath or Cruelty represented by a crouching, bearded brute attacking a half-grown youngster with a dagger; Despair tearing her hair; Envy eating her own entrails; and Avarice with her purse. On the extreme right, a woman in a dark hood, who can be identified as Tribulation, enters upon the scene from the outside rather than as if released from the box, and threatens Pandora with two hammers; she symbolizes something like remorse, "the gloomy and black thoughts that mortify the soul and heart as though they were hammers torturing it with continuous blows." [3]

17. *Pandora Opening the Box*
Printer's mark of Gourbin

Rosso's drawing is generally and correctly dated in the last period of his life (1530–1540), which he spent at the court of Francis I, and the presence of the crow even establishes 1534—or, if he used the Paris rather than the second Augsburg edition of the *Emblemata*, 1536—as a *terminus ante quem non*. Small wonder that the only direct if unspectacular effect of Rosso's composition can be observed in France: the Parisian publisher Gilles Gourbin or

[3] Ripa, *Iconologia, s.v.* "Tribulatione," where the figure is described as holding three hammers in one hand; Rosso seems to have reduced their number to two, one held in each hand, in order to lend greater verisimilitude and force to the action. That the idea was current in the first half of the sixteenth century is proved by Jörg Pencz's engraving B. 36, a bookplate executed for Willibald Pirckheimer in 1529, where Tribulatio hammers a heart held into the fire by Invidia while Toleratio reclines in the foreground and Spes points to heaven with a comforting forefinger; for a preparatory drawing formerly ascribed to Dürer (L. 299), see E. Panofsky, *Albrecht Dürer*, Princeton, 1943, 1945, 1948, II, p. 144, No. 1529.

Gorbin (in business from 1555 to 1586), who may have acquired the drawing, or a copy thereof, after the master's death, adopted the central figure,
changed only in minor details and still accompanied by her faithful crow, for

18. *Pandora Opening the Box*
Printer's mark of Gourbin

three different versions of his printer's mark, one of them large, the other two
small (*figs. 17* and *18*).[4] Operating in a house named À l'Espérance (near
the Collège de Cambrai),[5] he hailed Rosso's Pandora as a humanistic symbol

[4] See L. C. Silvestre, *Marques typographiques
. . . en France . . . depuis 1470 jusqu'à la fin
du seizième siècle*, Paris, 1867, ɪ, p. 252, No.
462, p. 334, No. 609; ɪɪ, p. 676, No. 1165.

[5] See P. Delalain, *Inventaire des marques
d'imprimeurs et de libraires*, Paris, 1892, p. 40,
correctly explaining Gourbin's reasons for
adopting Pandora as his printer's mark but
mistaking the crow for a dove.

19. RENÉ BOYVIN AFTER ROSSO FIORENTINO: *L'Ignorance chassée*

of Hope and selected as a motto half a line from Niccolò della Valle's translation of Hesiod: "Spes Sola Remansit Intus."

Originally, however, Rosso's drawing would seem to have been intended
for a purpose quite different from that of furnishing the model for a *marque
d'imprimeur:* it was made, we believe, in preparation for one of Rosso's own
big frescoes in the Galerie François Premier at Fontainebleau, commonly
known as *L'Ignorance chassée* but better designated *Francis I Overcoming
the Evils of Ignorance (fig. 19).*[6]

Like Dürer's famous engraving *Knight, Death, and Devil,* this composition lends expression to the ideal formulated in Erasmus of Rotterdam's
Enchiridion militis Christiani. "Undiverted by the blandishments of the
world," the Christian knight ignores all vices and temptations as though they
were mere "spooks and phantoms" ("terricula et phantasmata") and passes
them by as though they were not there, "steadily fixing his mind on the thing
itself and always remembering the Lord's 'Look not behind thee.' "[7] But
where Dürer's hero is an anonymous representative of Christian fortitude,
Rosso's is Francis I, King of France. Where the former strives to reach the
Fortress of Faith, the latter triumphantly enters the Gates of Jupiter, identified as such by the inscription *Ostium Iovis.* And where the former is contrasted with the negative symbols of Christian eschatology, Death and the
Devil, the latter is contrasted with the negative symbols of Socratic ethics
(even though some of the figures are still reminiscent of the Capital Sins):[8]
a seething mass of Vices born of Ignorance, and therefore blindfolded. The

---

[6] Kusenberg, *op. cit.,* pp. 69 f., Plate xLvi; Barocchi, *op. cit.,* pp. 128 f., figs. 84–86 (il-lustrating the fresco itself as well as Boyvin's engraving reproduced in our *fig. 19*). Barocchi, p. 128, justly emphasizes the similarity in temperament that exists between this composi-tion and the Pandora drawing. For the ex-tensive literature on Fontainebleau, see now the useful bibliography appended to F. Bo-logna's and R. Causa's catalogue of *Fontaine-bleau e la maniera italiana (Mostra d'Oltre-mare e del lavoro italiano del mondo,* Naples, July 26–Oct. 12, 1952), Florence, 1952.

[7] Cf. E. Panofsky, *Albrecht Dürer,* pp. 141 ff. Erasmus was highly appreciated by Francis I, who, through Budé, made the greatest efforts to entice him to Paris in 1517–1518.

[8] The youth laying his hands upon the breast and buttocks of a slender nude obviously repre-sents the vice of luxury (cf. Bronzino's well-known *Exposure of Luxury* in the National Gallery at London), while the figure huddled in front of the gates may be identified with Despair, and the mother carrying a child with Pride, "Aroganza, matre de ogni male."

fresco thus anticipates the tribute paid by Joachim du Bellay to Francis I after his passing:

> *C'est luy qui a de ce beau siecle ici*
> *Comme un soleil, tout obscur eclairci,*
> *Ostant aux yeux des bons espriz de France*
> *Le noir bandeau de l'aveugle ignorance.*[9]

20. *Ex utroque Caesar*

From Paradin, *Symbola heroica*

Furthermore, to glorify the king as a ruler no less solicitous for the flowering of arts and letters than for military success, Rosso has placed a sword in his hand and a book under his arm. Instead of being a *Miles Christianus* and nothing else, he is "ex utroque Caesar," and it is in fact in connection with a regal figure obviously derived from the portrayal of Francis I in the *Ignorance chassée* that this proverbial phrase (later more generally quoted as "*in utroque Caesar*") seems to occur for the first time (*fig. 20*).[10]

The Erasmian spirit of Rosso's allegory, glorifying sovereign disdain for evil [11] rather than its conquest through active op-

---

[9] Joachim du Bellay, *La Louange du feu Roy François et du Treschrestien Roy Henry*, 5 ff. (first edition, Paris, 1549; H. Chamard, ed., *Joachim du Bellay, Oeuvres poétiques*, III, Paris, 1912, p. 142). See also the same poet's *Salutation prosphonégmatique au Roy Treschrestien Henry II* (first edition, Paris, 1549; Chamard, *ibidem*, p. 70).

Comment te peut assez chanter la France,
O grand François, des neuf Seurs adoré?
Tu as defaict ce vil monstre Ignorance,
Tu as refaict le bel aage doré.

It seems in fact that French Renaissance poets could hardly mention the name of Francis I without extolling him as the conqueror of Ignorance, as when du Bellay expresses his fears that, eleven years after the passing of the "grand François," "Phoebus s'en fuit de nous, & l'antique ignorance / Sous la faveur de Mars

retourne encore en France" (*Les Regrets*, 1558, Chamard, *op. cit.*, II, 1910, p. 202; E. Droz, ed., *Joachim du Bellay, Les Antiquitez de Rome et Les Regrets*, Paris, 1945, p. 152). Cf. also the passages quoted below, p. 48, note. The excellent Abbé C. P. Goujet, *Mémoires historiques & littéraires sur le College Royal de France*, Paris, 1758, I, p. 239 f., says very nicely that the *Ignorance chassée* "désigne clairement le zèle que François I. témoigna pour le rétablissement des Lettres en France & qu'il effectua principalement par la Fondation du College Royal."

[10] Claude Paradin, *Devises héroiques*. The first edition (Lyons, 1551) was not accessible to us. Our *fig. 20* is reproduced from the Latin translation (*Symbola heroica*, Antwerp, 1583), p. 284, where the explanation reads as follows: "Hoc apophthegmate: *Ex utroque Caesar*, significatur, his duobus, armis scilicet

et literis, Iulium Caesarem recto corporis statu semper rebus gerendis strenue invigilantem, factum totius orbis dominatorem." With the motto "Ex utroque Caesar" inscribed on luxuriant scrollwork, Paradin's emblem is repeated in G. Symeoni, *Dialogo dell'imprese militari et morali* (first edition, Lyons, 1559), Lyons, 1574, p. 183; and it recurs, under the headline "A *Princes* Most Ennobling Parts / Are Skill in *Armes* and Love to *Arts*," in George Wither, *A Collection of Emblems Ancient and Moderne*, London, 1635, I, 32, the picture showing an emperor with a sword in his right hand and an open book in his left. In form, the later proverbial phrase may have been patterned after such locutions as Cicero's "Quorum generum [*scil.*, vel ad hortandum vel ad docendum] *in utroque magnus*" (*De legibus*, III, 18, 40, with reference to Cato). In content, it can be traced back to the beginning of Justinian's *Institutiones:* "Imperatoriam maiestatem non solum armis decoratam, sed etiam legibus oportet esse armatam, ut *utrumque tempus* et bellorum et pacis recte possit gubernari . . . Quorum *utramque viam* . . . adnuente deo perfecimus." That this derivation (suggested to us by Professor E. H. Kantorowicz) was known to the emblematists themselves is confirmed by the fact that the emblem of the German Emperor Frederick III (a book and sword, inscribed "Hic regit, illa tuetur") was explained in the following manner: "Leges & arma in promptu habes, illae regunt, haec tuentur imperium; a Justiniano habet Imperator Fridericus, ut sine quibus Imperatores, non modo Imperium, sed ne nomen quidem tueri possent" (*Jacobi Typotii Symbola Divina et Humana Pontificum, Imperatorum, Regum*, Arnheim, 1668, pp. 118 f.). Without the reference to Justinian this emblem also occurs in Silvestro Petrasanta, *De symbolis heroicis*, Antwerp, 1634, p. 224, as well as in Wither, *loc. cit.*, I, 3 (here, characteristically, with the Tablets of the Law substituted for the book); two related emblems ascribed, respectively, to Rudolph I of Germany and Philip the Fair of France are found in Typotius, *op. cit.*, pp. 103 f. and 230 f.: an arm holding a mace and an olive branch, inscribed *Utrum lubet*, and a sword crossed *per saltire* with a palm, inscribed *Utrumque*. Needless to say, Cesare Ripa did not fail to make use of the conceit in his *Iconologia*. His personification of Merit (*Merito*) is represented with one arm encased in armor and the other bare,

the hand of the former holding a scepter as a symbol of "warlike action," the other a book as a symbol of "lo studio e le opere delle lettere." The personification of Government (*Governo della reppublica*) is described as equipped, in order to express the same idea, with an olive branch and a spear or arrow (*dardo*) but not illustrated. It should be noted, however, that the humanism of the Renaissance transformed the original contrast between *arma* and *leges*, arms and law, into a contrast between *arma* and *literae*, arms and learning. Even before Rosso's fresco and the emblem books a figure bearing a sword and a book was used as a personification of virtue as opposed to pleasure in Raphael's charming *Dream of Scipio* in the Musée Condé at Chantilly, and it was especially in France (and Spain) that a happy union of "arms and letters" was proclaimed as an ideal solution of the problem, not only of government, but of human endeavor in general (cf. E. R. Curtius, *Europäische Literatur und lateinisches Mittelalter*, Bern, 1948, pp. 183 ff., particularly 185 f.): in 1575 Louis Le Roy published his important work, *De la vicissitude ou Variété des choses en l'univers et concurrence des armes et des lettres . . .*, which is largely based upon the premise that the arts and war develop hand in hand (see H. Weisinger, "Louis Le Roy on Science and Progress," *Osiris*, XI, 1954, p. 199 ff.). As time went on, this new ideal underwent a further change. In a later French version of Paradin's work, published at Paris in 1621 under the title *Devises héroiques*, p. 152, the "Ex utroque Caesar" emblem is replaced by a new one, entitled "In utrumque paratus," which consists of two hands, one holding a sword, the other a mason's trowel; this is explained by the story of the people of Israel, which, after their return from the Babylonian captivity, "fut constraint de bâtir de l'une des mains et tenir l'espée de l'autre," and is compared to the Church in its double function of instruction and self-defense. The concept of law (or peace), then, is successively replaced by the concepts of learning and religion.

[11] An interesting survival of this idea can be seen in a French tapestry, preserved in the Speed Art Museum at Louisville, Kentucky (*fig. 21*), where Louis XIV, accompanied by two dignitaries, turns his back upon a group of such Evils as Avarice, Envy, Impiety, and even Horace's Necessity (with hammer and nails).

position, becomes particularly evident when we compare his fresco with what must be considered its most important pictorial sources: two composi-

21. Louis XIV Turning His Back upon the Vices

tions by Mantegna, which, from a purely iconographical point of view, may be considered counterparts and are so closely interrelated that many of the same personifications and symbols occur in both.

One is the famous *Expulsion of the Vices from the Grove of Virtue*, painted for Isabella d'Este's *studiolo* at Mantua and now preserved in the

22. Andrea Mantegna: *Expulsion of the Vices*

Louvre (*fig. 22*).[12] Here a warlike Minerva, fortified by the celestial apparition of Justice, Fortitude, and Temperance and possibly herself representing

[12] See R. Förster, "Studien zu Mantegna und den Bildern im Studierzimmer der Isabella Gonzaga," *Jahrbuch der königlich Preussischen Kunstsammlungen*, XXII, 1901, pp. 78 ff.; P. Kristeller, *Mantegna* (English translation), London, New York, and Bombay, p. 356 ff.; E. Wind, *Bellini's "Feast of the Gods,"* Cambridge (Mass.), 1948, pp. 17 ff., Plates 47, 48.

the fourth moral virtue, Prudence,[13] rushes forth to free the Grove of Virtue—
the latter represented in the guise of a Daphnelike crossbreed of laurel tree
and human figure [14]—from the invasion of the Vices, who flee in disorder. The
other is a composition, transmitted by two engravings formerly ascribed to
Zoan Andrea, that may be entitled *The Fall and Rescue of Foolish Humanity*
(*fig. 23*).[15] In this case, Virtue, again represented as a humanized laurel tree,
has been abandoned (*Virtus deserta*) or destroyed by fire (*Virtus combusta*)
so that the Vices have conquered her realm in perpetuity. A woman is about
to be thrown into a pit by personifications of incomprehension and luxury, to
join a heap of other unfortunates already wriggling in the pit; they can be
rescued, however, provided that they want to be rescued, by the ministrations
of Mercury, the god of logic, learning, and eloquence.

That Rosso knew these two compositions can hardly be questioned. His
Ignorance chassée, with Francis I taking the place of Minerva (who in Mantegna's Louvre picture stands, of course, for Isabella d'Este),[16] is reminiscent
of this painting in general arrangement and even in such details as the direct
juxtaposition of the hero with a woman carrying a baby in her arms; on the
other hand, it resembles the "Zoan Andrea" engravings in the prevalence of
nudity and blindfolded faces. With both compositions, however, it shares the
dominant idea of its iconography and, even more revealing, the physical char-
acterization of the chief antagonist of Virtue, Ignorance herself. Mantegna
(whose favorite saying is reported to have been "Virtuti semper adversatur
ignorantia")[17] as well as Rosso tried to express the—fundamentally unchris-

---

[13] Thus Wind, *loc. cit.* At the same time, Minerva must be taken to be a glorified por-trayal of Isabella d'Este herself; it should be remembered that Marguerite de Navarre was to be praised, in perfectly analogous fashion, as a "Pallas armed against Ignorance" ("Pal-las contre l'ignorance armée") by François de Billon; see E. Bourciez, *Les Moeurs polies et la littérature de cour sous Henri* II, Paris, 1886, p. 151.

[14] The tree is enveloped by a scroll inscribed, in Latin, Greek, and Hebrew: "Onward, divine companions of the Virtues, who return to us from on high; drive from our seas these foul monsters of the Vices."

[15] See Förster, *op. cit., passim*; Kristeller, *op. cit.*, p. 374; Wind, *op. cit.*, pp. 17 ff., Plate 47. A conclusive survey of the earlier literature and an excellent reproduction is found in A. M. Hind, *Early Italian Engraving*, v, 2, London, 1948, pp. 27 ff., No. 22, Plate 520.

[16] See above, n. 13.

[17] See Förster, *op. cit.*, p. 86; Hind, *loc. cit.*

23. AFTER
ANDREA MANTEGNA:
Virtus combusta
and *Virtus deserta*

tian—idea that ignorance rather than wickedness, not knowing what is right rather than not willing what is right, is the cause of all evil: Οὐδεὶς ἑκὼν ἁμαρτάνει, "No one sins willingly," as Socrates is believed to have said.[18] Now, both in the Louvre picture and in the "Zoan Andrea" engravings, Ignorance is represented in identical fashion: as an inordinately fat and disgustingly androgynous figure, crowned but blind (Mantegna makes a well-

[18] For the occurrence of this "Socratic paradox" in Plato's writings, see the collection of passages in P. Shorey, *What Plato Said*, Chicago, 1933, p. 640. Cf. also Diogenes Laërtius, *De vitis . . . clarorum philosophorum*, II, 5, 14: ἔλεγε δὲ [Σωκράτης] καὶ ἓν μόνον ἀγαθὸν εἶναι, τὴν ἐπιστήμην, καὶ ἓν μόνον κακὸν, τὴν ἀμαθίαν.

considered distinction between the state of actual blindness, denoting the permanent absence of sight, and the state of being merely blindfolded, denoting the temporary absence of sight), and incapable of movement: "O thou monster Ignorance, how deformed dost thou look!" [19] In the Louvre picture this repulsive being—which would seem to owe its sexual ambiguity and several of its features and attributes to Mantegna's fusing of Ignorantia pure and simple (cf. *fig. 23*) with Plutus, the god of riches [20]—is shown defeated. Unable to walk but the first to retreat, she is carried away by two ancillary Vices, Avarice and Ingratitude, leaving the Grove of Virtue, as yet undefaced, to the liberating forces of Minerva. In the engravings, the fat crowned monster is triumphant and firmly entrenched: the realm of a Virtue "deserted" or "burned" is reduced to desolation, and Ignorance, here having appropriated the attributes of Fortune in addition to those of Plutus, rules supreme. She rests her arm on Fortune's rudder and sits, as if enthroned, on Fortune's sphere, which is supported—and, as it were, stabilized—by the symbols of ignorance and wealth, two sphinxes and a purse.[21] It is from this "Ignorantia-Plutus," devised by Mantegna,[22] that Rosso developed the colossal figure that

[19] Shakespeare, *Love's Labour's Lost*, IV, 2, 23. Cf. the passages from du Bellay quoted in n. 9, p. 40, and p. 48, note.

[20] Cf. below, n. 22 and *fig. 24*.

[21] For the sphinx as a symbol of ignorance, see, e.g., Alciati, *Emblemata*, Emblem CLXXXVII (in the later editions): "Quod monstrum id? Sphinx est. Cur candida virginis ora? Et volucrum pennas, crura leonis habet? / Hanc faciem assumpsit rerum ignorantia: tanti / Scilicet est triplex caussa et origo mali." Claudius Minos adduces as a source a passage from the *Tabula Cebetis* (also exploited by Natale Conti, *op. cit.*, IX, 18, p. 1007), where the sphinx is identified with Ἀφροσύνη.

[22] To develop a fixed iconographical type for the representation of Ignorance had not been necessary until, probably on Leon Battista Alberti's recommendation, numerous artists of the Renaissance attempted to reconstruct *The Calumny of Apelles* as described by Lucian (see R. Förster, "Die Verleumdung des Apelles in der Renaissance," *Jahrbuch der königlich Preussischen Kunstsammlungen*, VII, 1887, pp. 29 ff., 89 ff.; G. A. Giglioli, "La Calumnia di

Apelle," *Rassegna d'arte*, VII, 1920, pp. 173 ff.). For here the stupid, donkey-eared judge had to be shown enthroned between two bad advisors, Suspicio and Ignorantia. In the earliest *Calumny* that has come down to us, Botticelli's famous picture in the Uffizi, the characteristics of Ignorance are not as yet very marked: she is a youngish, not bad-looking woman distinguished only by a general lack of animation, drooping eyelids, and a sagging mouth. But in Mantegna's redaction—transmitted by a possibly authentic drawing in the British Museum (*fig. 24*) and an engraving by Girolamo Mocetto (B. 10, Hind, *op. cit.*, V, 2, pp. 165 f., No. 12, Plate 727)—she has acquired three definite characteristics, which, as is shown in the text, she shares with the analogous figures in both the Louvre picture (*fig. 22*) and the "Zoan Andrea" engravings (*fig. 23*): she is inordinately fat, she has no eyes, and she has a crown.

The first two of these traits are borrowed from Plutus, the god of riches. Always closely associated with Ignorance (according to Aristophanes, Zeus himself had deprived him

24. Andrea Mantegna: *The Calumny of Apelles*

of his eyes "so that he might be unable to distinguish between good and evil people" in bestowing his favors), Plutus had become a familiar figure through the rediscovery of Lucian's witty dialogue, *Timon* (converted into an Italian comedy, dedicated to Isabella d'Este's brother, by Bojardo: *Timone; Commedia del Magnifico Conte Matheo Maria Bojardo . . . Tradutta di uno Dialogo di Luciano a complacentia dello Illustrissimo Principe Signor Hercule Estense Duca di Ferrara,* Venice, 1518), and here the god paints his own portrait in very clear and unflattering terms. He is not only blind but eyeless; he becomes fatter and larger every day if locked up in a dark dungeon; he is associated with Evil and Ignorance; and when the doors of a house are opened to him, there enter, together with him, "in a kind of masquerade, Pride, Folly, Madness, Sloth, Contumely, Deceit, and six hundred other attendants of the same quality." This, then, accounts for both the blindness and the obesity of Ignorance. However, Plutus, god of wealth, tended to be confused, even in classical antiquity, with Pluto, god of the nether world; in fact, the Greek name Πλοῦτος is a euphemism actually designating the latter as "rich." (Boccaccio, *Genealogia deorum,* VIII, 4 and 6, sanctioned the confusion; Lan-

dino, in his *Commentary* on Dante's *Inferno,* VII, writes: "Vogliono che [Plutone] ancora sia Dio delle ricchezze . . . le ricchezze sempre tirano l'animo humano alle cose vile & basse," and such mythographers as Vincenzo Cartari and Natale Conti had a hard time keeping the two characters apart.) And Pluto, as king of all the souls in Hades, was entitled to a crown, a fact especially stressed, e.g., by Martianus Capella and, after him, by Cartari (*Imagini dei Dei degli antichi,* Venice edition of 1621, p. 277). So, as the sightlessness and fatness of Ignorance in Mantegna's *Calumny of Apelles* resulted from her equation with Plutus, so can her crown, thus far unexplained, be accounted for by the latter's equation with Pluto.

Once crowned, Mantegna's Ignorance remained a "queen" in his *Expulsion of the Vices (fig. 22)* as well as in his *Fall and Rescue of Foolish Humanity,* transmitted through the "Zoan Andrea" engravings *(fig. 23).* But in these two compositions she borrowed a further feature from Lucian's portrait of the god of riches: his inability to walk. "I knew long before," Plutus is addressed, "that you were blind but never dreamt that you were lame into the bargain." "I cannot apprehend how it happens," Plutus replies, "but I am slow-paced and lame on both feet." (Rosso,

dominates and unifies the group of Vices in the Fontainebleau fresco, a figure equally stupid, equally incapable of normal movement, equally fat, and equally androgynous; he departed from his model only in that he represented her blindfolded rather than blind, showed her painfully supporting herself on a staff rather than carried by subsidiary personifications, and deprived her of her crown, which, in his opinion, had to remain the prerogative of the king.

Seen as a whole, however, Rosso's group of Vices, its elements governed by an explosively centrifugal impulse and its contour broken by projecting arms and hands, emphatically differs from everything envisaged by Mantegna or, for that matter, from Rosso's other compositions in the Galerie François Premier. But it resembles, no less emphatically, his Pandora drawing. And since this similarity extends to content as well as form—we have in both cases a group of desperate, wildly gesticulating Vices arrayed around a pivotal figure embodying their *raison d'être*, which is nescience in the case of Ignorance and curiosity in the case of Pandora—we are faced with the question whether a direct connection exists between the drawing and the fresco.

That this question must be answered in the affirmative is indicated, we believe, by a motif mentioned, but not as yet discussed, above: the Gates of Jupiter, which are so important a feature in the *Ignorance chassée*. These

---

needless to say, alluded to the same deficiency by equipping Ignorance with that staff on which she painfully supports herself.) And when, in the "Zoan Andrea" engravings, the attributes of Ignorance, here shown triumphant, are further augmented by those of Fortune, this final complication is justified by the fact that Fortune fully shares the prejudices of Wealth: "It is believed," says Cartari (p. 283), "that Plutus is quick and fast in bringing riches to the scoundrels and walks hesitantly and slowly when conveying them to good people, which is also a property of Fortune; and Pausanias praises the clever idea of him who, at Thebes, placed the god Plutus in the hands of Fortune, the latter being, as it were, the former's mother and nurse [cf. Pausanias, *Periëgesis*, IX, 16, 2]."

For the concept of Ignorance in French humanism, see, apart from du Bellay's brief reference to the "vil monstre Ignorance" (n. 9, p. 40), the same poet's comprehensive description in *La Musagnoeomachie*, 37 ff. (first edition, Paris, 1550; Chamard, *op. cit.*, IV, 1919, p. 5 ff.). Here Ignorance is described as lying in a cave and vomiting green bile. She has long, pointed ears like a donkey's and "levres tortues" like a lion's, and her hairy paws, "qui trainent ses membres lourds, / Immitent les pas d'un ours." She rolls her heavy body "comme une taupe aveuglée." While supporting "many a victorious scepter and many a sacred crown," she is the parent of Fraud, False Counsel, Discord, Ambition, Pride, Calumnious Envy, Cruelty, Malice, Avarice, and Sloth. And it is again Francis I who, by divine retribution, chases this *malheur aveuglé* over the plains of France.

25. Jean Cousin: *Fata Homerica*

gates are flanked by two gigantic vases inscribed *Boni* and *Mali*, a motif derived from Homer's *Iliad*, XXIV, 527:

> *Two Tuns with Lots stand at Jove's Pallas Gates,*
> *From whence he draws our good and evil Fates.*
> *Those worser he with better fortune blends,*
> *Them one day hurts, another makes amends;*
> *Who only bad encounter, wander hurl'd*
> *In want by Gods and Mortals round the World.*[23]

[23] John Ogilby's translation of 1669, London. Partly, perhaps, through the influence of Rosso's fresco, the motif of the two pithoi standing before the Gates of Jupiter became extremely popular in emblem books, and quite particularly on French soil. In his *Livre de Fortune* of 1568 Jean Cousin illustrated the *Fata Homerica* in naïvely naturalistic fashion (fig. 25): Jupiter, a thunderbolt in either hand, is shown seated between two big wooden wine casks inscribed *Boni* and *Mali* (L. Lalanne, *Le Livre de Fortune de Jean Cousin*, Paris, 1883, Plate CXXV). In Jean-Jacques Boissard's *Emblemata* the representation (fig. 26)

In these lines, then, we have the pithos motif in duplicate, so to speak, and commentators would not have been commentators had they not tried to

26. *Fata Homerica*
From Boissard, *Emblematum Liber*

correlate Jupiter's two pithoi, one containing good and the other evil, with Pandora's one pithos, containing evil alone.

This correlation, frowned upon by modern scholarship,[24] is, or at least appears to be, implied by as early a writer as Plutarch, who, in his *Letter of Condolence to Apollonius*, quotes Hesiod's account (*Works and Days*, 94–

---

is brought up to humanistic standards by the substitution of more authentic-looking vessels, looking like hydriae minus handles and inscribed καλόν and κακόν, for the wooden casks inscribed *Boni* and *Mali*; at the same time the classical idea of Fate is fused with the Christian contrast between the "green tree" and the "dry tree" (Iani Iacobi Boissardi Vesuntini, *Emblematum Liber*, Metz, 1588, p. 31; the first edition, Metz, 1584, was not accessible to us). In Bocchi's *Symbolicae Quaestiones*, finally, the pithoi are transformed into handsome *oinochoai*, and the idea is cleverly varied in that only the vessel of good is entrusted to Jupiter, whereas the vessel of evil has been appropriately turned over to malevolent Saturn, and in that a handsome genius represents the happy medium between the two extremes (Bocchi, *op. cit.*, I, 7, p. xvi, our *fig. 27*).

[24] See, for example, U. von Wilamowitz-Möllendorff, *Hesiodos' Erga*, Berlin, 1928, p. 52; Harrison, *op. cit.*, p. 105, n. 1; Pauly-Wissowa, *op. cit.*, XVIII, 3, cols. 539 ff., 546.

103) of Pandora's πιθοιγία (opening of the vessel) directly after Homer's description of the Gates of Jupiter (*Iliad*, XXIV, 522–533) and effects a transition by the words: "Hesiod . . . *also* confines the evils in a great urn and

27. GIULIO BONASONE: *Fata Homerica*

represents Pandora as opening it."[25] It was endorsed by the most respected commentators on Homer as well as Hesiod, Eustathius and Proclus,[26] and did

[25] Plutarch, *Moralia*, 105, D, E: . . . 'Ησίοδος, καὶ οὗτος ἐν πίθῳ κατείρξας τὰ κακὰ, τὴν Πανδώρην ἀνοίξασαν ἀποφαίνει. Plutarch's *Moralia* appeared in a French translation by Jacques Amyot in 1572. Here (*Oeuvres de Plutarque, Traduction du Grec par Jacques Amyot*, X, Paris, 1784, p. 328) the word πίθος is rendered as *tonneau*.

[26] For the interpretation of the Homer passage, see *Eustathii Archiepiscopi Thessaloniensis Commentaria ad Homeri Iliadem*, Leipzig, 1827, pp. 368 f.; for that of Hesiod's *Works and Days*, 94, see Proclus as printed in Gaisford, *op. cit.*, p. 86: "Εστι μὲν ὁ πίθος ἡ μία δύναμις τῆς Εἱμαρμένης, ἡ πάντων τῶν ἀπονεμομένων ταῖς πεσούσαις εἰς τὴν γένεσιν

not fail to impress the humanists of the Renaissance. Caelius Rhodiginus, a personal protégé of Francis I, asserted that the "vat of Pandora [*Pandorae dolium*] indicates the power of fate, which distributes *good and evil* among the souls about to be born" and draws attention to the fact that Hesiod himself calls this fate the "mind of *Zeus*." [27] In the poem accompanying a print (*fig. 38*) by the Dutch engraver Pieter Serwouters (1586–1657) Pandora's box— here looking rather like a little saucepan—is described as "the bridal gift of the gods wherein Jove had enclosed both good and evil" [28]—a notion that, as will be remembered, is foreign to all classical accounts of the Pandora myth. And, most important, the great Joachim du Bellay, philosophizing about *Les Misères et fortunes humaines*, proceeds exactly like Plutarch in linking the vases at the Gates of Jupiter to the vase of Pandora, even though he, a good Erasmian, had learned to think of the latter as a *boëte* while visualizing the former as *deux tonneaux:*

> *Le nombre est petit de ceux ores*
> *Qui sont les bien aymez des Dieux,*
> *Et ceux que la vertu encores*
> *Ardente a elevez aux cieux.*

> *Jupiter tient devant sa porte*
> *Deux tonneaux, dont il fait pluvoir*

ψυχαῖς χωρητικὴ καλλιόνων ἢ χειρόνων, δι᾽ ἃ εὔμοιροί τινές εἰσιν ἢ κακόμοιροι. Περιέχει γὰρ οὗτος τοὺς, παρ᾽ Ὁμήρῳ δύο πίθους, τοὺς τῶν κηρῶν πλήρεις.

[27] *Ludovici Caelii Rhodigini lectionum antiquarum libri* XVI, Basel, 1517, IV, 20, p. 182 (*idem, Lectionum antiquarum libri triginta,* Frankfurt and Leipzig, 1666, VII, 20, col. 361 ff.): "*Pithos* autem, hoc est Pandorae dolium, fati potentiam indicat. Quae prodeuntibus ad generationem animis bona distribuit vel mala [cf. the Proclus passage quoted in the preceding note]. . . . Sed hoc ipsum [*scil., fatum*] vocat Hesiodus Διὸς νοῦν id est, Iovis mentem" (also quoted in Guillaume de la Perrière's *Théâtre des bons engins,* published and dedicated to Marguerite de Navarre in 1539). It was by the personal intervention of Francis I that Caelius Rho-

diginus was appointed, in 1515, professor of Greek and Latin literature at Milan University, which position he held up to 1521.

[28] The Dutch inscription of Serwouters' engraving (for its iconography, cf. below, pp. 80 ff.) reads, in translation, about as follows: "Behold here how the joyous son of Maia entrusts Pandora to Epimetheus, and she, eager to look, opens her bridal gift from the gods: the golden box wherein Jupiter had enclosed good and evil all together so that man might have no reason to complain and might enjoy a sufficiency all his days. But, alas, the virtues fly into the air and mischief stays below, over which mankind still sighs. Epimetheus must pay the price for this action of the stupid woman, and his one and only salvation is Hope."

Tout ce qui aux humains aporte
De quoy ayse ou tristesse avoir.

Qui a veu en ce vieil poëte
(Et le voyant, ne pleure lors)
La trop tost ouverte boëte,
Et les vertuz volants dehors?

L'esperance au bord arrestée
Outre son gré demeure icy:
Puis que seule nous est prestée,
Gardon' qu'ell' ne s'en vole aussi.[29]

If, only a few years after the composition of the Galerie François Premier, the mind of an educated Frenchman automatically associated Pandora's box with the two vessels in front of the *Ostium Iovis,* we are entitled to assume that Rosso's Pandora drawing was conceived and executed in connection with the *Ignorance chassée* fresco (where this *Ostium Iovis* plays such a prominent role), either as a design for one of the stucco cartouches, which are often related to the large pictures much as a footnote is to the main text, or, perhaps more probably, as a design for a section of the fresco itself: the Pandora scene, so similar to the present group of Vices even in such details as the outstretched arms of the figure next to the heroine, may well have been destined to take the place now occupied by this very group. The ruling idea of the fresco is to show how, after Evil had come into the world, the king, and only the king, is able to conquer, or rather to transcend, it. But as to the origin of Evil itself, a preliminary plan may well have been based upon the pseudo-classical notion according to which the evils contained in one of Jupiter's pithoi are transmitted to earth by Pandora and are there released by her

[29] Du Bellay, *Vers lyriques,* II (first edition, Paris, 1549; Chamard, *op. cit.,* III, 1912, pp. 10 f.). For the fact that the motif of Jupiter's pithoi was current in France as late as the eighteenth century and was still automatically associated with the Pandora myth, see Voltaire's letter to J.-B. de Laborde, referred to below, p. 120, n. 6. In making Virtues rather than Vices escape from the box, du Bellay follows, of course, Babrius; cf. above, p. 8, and below, pp. 82 ff.

improvidence, rather than upon the authentic classical notion that they are born of ignorance.

That the Pandora motif was subsequently abandoned in favor of the ignorance theme can be accounted for, we think, by two considerations. First, it may have seemed advisable not to deflect the beholder's attention from the triumphant but inconspicuous figure of the king to an action as stirring and spectacular as that of Pandora. Second, the very atmosphere of Francis I's court may have inspired a change from the Judaeo-Christian idea—sin originates from curiosity—to the Socratic notion, expressed in Mantegna's allegories, that sin results from ignorance. Francis I was, for all his faults, a sincere admirer and protector of humanism and expected much, perhaps too much, from "education." Under the guidance of his great Guillaume Budé he planned, as early as 1517–1518, a "Collège des Trois Langues" (Hebrew, Latin, and Greek), which, just when Rosso made his appearance at the French court, was formally established as the Collège de France; and he collected a library, originally kept at Fontainebleau, that was especially rich in the Greek classics. We can easily see that in this humanistic climate Ignorance won out over Pandora. Pandora is, in spite of her Hellenic origin, a sister of Eve rather than Ἀφροσύνη. And this leads us to her next major adventure in Renaissance art.

V

Roma Prima Pandora; Eva Prima Pandora; Lutetia Nova Pandora

AN INTEREST in the Greek language and in Greek literature was, need-less to say, common to the entire Renaissance. In one respect, however, France was ahead even of Italy. Free from that nationalistic bias—fomented by Petrarch—which made the Italians think of themselves as direct descendants of the Romans and led them to extol everything Latin at the expense of everything Greek,[1] the French looked by and large upon the Greek classics with even greater reverence than upon the Latin. Francis I, the founder of the Typographie Royale, appointed Conrad Néobar and, after the latter's death, Robert Estienne, for the special purpose of bringing out editions of the Greek classics surpassing those of Aldo Manucci (we still quote Plato and Plutarch by the pages of the editions published by Robert's son, Henri, who, though forced to spend most of his life at Geneva, must be regarded as a product of the French tradition).[2] And the French humanists, considering Greek litera-

---

[1] This was already observed by J. Burckhardt, *Die Kultur der Renaissance in Italien*, III, 3. In the tenth edition (Leipzig, 1908, I, pp. 366 f.) L. Geiger quotes some significant passages, for example, Enea Silvio Piccolomini ("Alphonsus, tanto es Socrate maior quanto gravior Romanus homo quam Graecus putatur") and Lorenzo Valla ("Eant igitur nunc Graeci, et linguarum copia se iactent; plus nostra una efficit . . . quam illorum quinque"). In contrast to this, Rabelais, *Gargantua et Pantagruel*, VIII, calls Greek a language "sans laquelle c'est honte qu'une personne se die sçavant."

[2] For the "Greek revival" in the French Renaissance in general and the printing activities of the Typographie Royale in particular, see E. Egger, *L'Hellénisme en France*, Paris, 1869, especially I, pp. 140 ff., 165 ff., 197 ff. (for the more recent literature on the "grecs du roi," cf. P. Hofer and G. W. Cottrell, "Angelos Vergecios and the Bestiary of Manuel Phile," *Harvard Library Bulletin*, VIII, 1954, pp. 323 ff., particularly p. 337); C. Terrasse, *François Iᵉʳ*,

ture a source of aesthetic enjoyment and inspiration as well as an object of philological study (one has a feeling that they were careful never to lose their "amateur standing"), did their best to make it accessible and palatable to the society in which they lived. They devoted, from the outset, a sustained effort to translating the Greek classics, particularly the great poets, into an elegant vernacular; and the first translator of Hesiod was none other than Jean Dorat, the "mentor of the Pléiade." [3] Thus we can easily conceive that Pandora, thoroughly Greek by birth and education, became in France—and, under French influence, in England and the Netherlands—what she was never to become in Italy and only at a much later date, and under different circumstances, in Germany: a living figure appealing to the imagination of writers and artists alike,[4] and from the outset understood as that consummate blend of blessing

---

II, Paris, 1948, particularly p. 336. The curiously Greek flavor of the French Renaissance can be sensed in such small symptoms as the fact that Ronsard—who celebrated Hugues Salel's translation of the *Iliad*, undertaken at the suggestion of Francis I, in a well-known poem—was praised as the "Pindare" rather than the "Virgile" or the "Horace français," and that he used *sortes Homericae* instead of the medieval *sortes Virgilianae* (P. de Nolhac, *Ronsard et l'humanisme*, Bibliothèque de l'École des Hautes Études, CCXXVII, Paris, 1921, pp. 124 f.).

[3] M. Augé-Chiquet, *La Vie, les idées et l'oeuvre de Jean-Antoine de Baïf*, Paris, 1909, p. 34, quotes Jacques Veillard's *Petri Ronsardi Poetae Gallici Laudatio Funebris*, Paris, 1586: "Hic Delius Auratus Aeschylum, Musaeum, Hesiodum Galliae donabat." In 1574 Jean-Antoine de Baïf himself published a translation of Hesiod's *Works and Days* in his *Etrénes de Poëzie Fransoëze* (C. Marty-Laveaux, ed., *La Pléiade Française*, XII, Paris, 1883, p. 328 ff.). His fanatical purism led him to call Pandora "Toutedon," and his translation of *Works and Days*, 94 ff., reads, in his strange phonetic orthography, as follows:

Mês la femél' autant de sa méin le kouvêrkle répandit
Haurs de la boêt' oz uméins douloureux maus k'éle proupant
Éspoêr seul kome dans kéke mêzon fort ă débrizér,

Reste léans aus bors de la boêt: é dehaurs ne vola pas.

In his *Du Naturel des femmes* (Marty-Laveaux, *op. cit.*, IX, 1881, p. 444) de Baïf retells the story of Pandora's endowment by the gods and calls her "ce beau mal" without, however, referring to the "boêt'."

For French translations from the Greek in general, see Egger, *loc. cit.*, especially, I, pp. 191 ff., 259 ff.; F. C. J. Hennebert, *Histoire des traductions françaises d'auteurs grecs et latins pendant le* XVIe *et le* XVIIe *siècles*, Brussels, 1861; M. Delcourt, *Étude sur les traductions des tragiques grecs et latins en France depuis la Renaissance* (Académie Royale de Belgique, Classe des Lettres, Mémoires, Coll. in octavo, 2 ser., XIX, 4, Brussels, 1925); cf. also Terrasse, *op. cit.*, pp. 329 ff. The international standing of the French translations is implicitly recognized by George Puttenham (*The Arte of English Poesie*, 1589, III, 22) when he blames John Soowthern for having translated Anacreon and Pindar from the French rather than the Greek.

[4] It is significant that a well-read French gentleman such as Blaise de Vigenère, when discussing a general reference to the creation of men by Prometheus, instinctively brings in Pandora: "Diodore refère la première invention des images aux Ethiopiens . . . & Lactance, au 2. liure de l'origine de l'erreur, chap. II, à Prométhée, qui fit sa Pandore d'argille & pour l'animer s'en alla desrober le feu dans

and curse which Hesiod had described in the immortal phrase καλὸν κακόν.

In the poems of Maurice Scève and Pierre Ronsard, Pandora could be used as a new and eloquent image of the lady beloved:

> *Le Naturant par ses haultes Idées*
> *Rendit de soy la Nature admirable.*
> *Par les vertus de sa vertu guidées*
> *S'esvertua en oeuvre esmerveillable.*
> *Car de tout bien, voyre es Dieux desirable,*
> *Parfeit un corps en sa parfection*
> *Mouvant aux Cieulx tel admiration*
> *Qu'au premier oeil mon ame l'adorat*
> *Comme de tous la delectation*
> *Et de moy seul fatale Pandora.*[5]

And:

> *Quand au premier la Dame que j'adore*
> *Vint embellir le sejour de noz cieulx,*
> *Le filz de Rhée appella tous les Dieux,*
> *Pour faire encor d'elle une aultre Pandore.*
> *Lors Apollin richement la decore,*
> *Or, de ses raiz luy façonnant les yeulx,*
> *Or, luy donnant son chant melodieux,*
> *Or, son oracle & ses beaulx vers encore.*
> *Mars luy donna sa fiere cruaulté,*
> *Venus son ris, Dione sa beaulté,*
> *Peithon sa voix, Ceres son abondance.*
> *L'Aube ses doigtz & ses crins deliez,*

---

le ciel" (*Philostrate: La description de Callistrate de quelques statues antiques*, Paris, 1615; here quoted from the edition of 1629, p. 852). Lactantius does not mention Pandora at all.

[5] Maurice Scève, *Délie, Object de plus haulte vertu*, Paris, 1544, II (E. Parturier, ed., Paris, 1916, p. 6). That the first eight lines of Scève's *dizain* rephrase Petrarch's Sonnet 169 and further medievalize Petrarch's Christian Platonism by the introduction of the scholastic concept of *natura naturans* (cf. the fine analysis by L. Spitzer, "The Poetic Treatment of a Platonic-Christian Theme," *Comparative Literature*, VI, 1954, p. 193, particularly p. 202, n. 11) makes the terminal evocation of the entirely unmedieval Pandora doubly remarkable.

Amour son arc, Thetis donna ses piedz,
Cleion sa gloyre, & Pallas sa prudence.[6]

In Joachim du Bellay's *Antiquitez de Rome*, however, this irresistible compound of good and evil became a symbol of the Eternal City: Pandora is Rome, and Rome is Pandora:

Tout le parfait dont le ciel nous honnore,
Tout l'imparfait qui naist dessous les cieux,
Tout ce qui paist noz esprits & nos yeux,
Et tout cela qui noz plaisirs devore:
Tout le malheur qui nostre aage dedore,
Tout le bon heur des siecles les plus vieux,
Rome *du temps de ses premiers ayeux*
Le tenoit clos, ainsi qu'une Pandore.
Mais le Destin débrouillant ce Chaos,
Ou tout le bien & le mal fut enclos,
A fait depuis que les vertus divines
Volant au ciel ont laissé les pechez,
Qui jusq' icy se sont tenus cachez
Sous les monceaux de ces vieilles ruines.[7]

The idea expressed in this sonnet and here made to glow, as it were, in the light of an intensely personal experience is, however, by no means unique;

[6] Pierre Ronsard, *Les Amours*, XXXII, Paris, 1552 (*Oeuvres complètes*, P. Laumonier, ed., Paris, IV, 1925, pp. 35 f.). In his commentary on this poem (1578) Marc-Antoine de Muret relates, after Hesiod, the story of Pandora at great length, correctly translating πίθος as *vase* but omitting the motif of Hope (Hugues Vaganay, *Oeuvres complètes de Ronsard: Les Amours de P. Ronsard commentées par Marc-Antoine de Muret* . . . , Paris, 1910, pp. 37 ff.).
[7] Joachim du Bellay, *Les Antiquitez de Rome*, XIX (first edition, 1558), Chamard, *op. cit.*, II, 1910, p. 19; Droz, *op. cit.*, p. 12. Edmund Spenser's translation (*Ruines of Rome*, XIX, here quoted after J. C. Smith and E. de Selincourt, eds., *The Poetical Works of Edmund Spenser*, London, etc., 1921, p. 512) reads as follows:

All that is perfect, which th' heauen beautifies,
All that's imperfect, borne belowe the Moone;
All that doth feede our spirits and our eies;
And all that doth consume our pleasures soone;
All the mishap, the which our daies outweares,
All the good hap of th' oldest times afore,
Rome in the time of her great ancestors,
Like a Pandora, locked long in store.
But destinie this huge Chaos turmoyling,
In which all good and euill was enclosed,
Their heauenly vertues from these woes assoyling,
Caried to heauen, from sinfull bondage losed:
But their great sinnes, the causers of their paine,
Vnder these antique ruines yet remaine.

by the middle of the sixteenth century the comparison, even equation, of a big city with Pandora seems to have been more or less current in French humanism. Even before it was applied to Rome by du Bellay—his *Antiquitez de Rome,* to be translated by Spenser, was published in 1558—it had been applied to Paris by the less distinguished scholars and poets who contrived the program for the *Entrée* of Henry II in 1549.

In sixteenth-century France the decorations and spectacles that solemnized the visits of kings to their principal cities acquired the character of Roman triumphs: the *entrée joyeuse* of the fifteenth century became an *entrée solennelle et triomphale.*[8] The processions, *tableaux vivants,* theatricals, and, above all, triumphal arches devised for these occasions teemed with classical gods, heroes, and personifications forced into the service of an adulation the like of which had hardly been seen since the days of the Roman Empire. Dorat explicitly instructed his pupils in the art of "properly hiding and concealing the classical fables and of disguising the truth of things with an imaginative cloak so as to immortalize the men whom the poet wishes to exalt and to praise."[9]

When the king entered a town, this town—acting as hostess, so to speak —had to be represented after the fashion of classical city personifications.

[8] See P. Champion, *Paris au temps de la Renaissance,* Paris, 1936; P. Le Vayer, *Les Entrées solennelles à Paris des rois et reines de France . . . conservées à la Bibliothèque Nationale,* Paris, 1896; J. Chartrou, *Les Entrées solennelles et triomphales à la Renaissance (1484–1551)*, Paris, 1928.

[9] Pierre Ronsard, *Hymne de l'Automne;* Laumonier, *op. cit.,* IV, p. 313 (quoted, e.g., in de Nolhac, *op. cit.,* p. 70):

> . . . je vins éstre
> *Disciple de Daurat, qui long temps fut mon maistre,*
> *M'apprist la Poësie & me monstra comment*
> *On doit feindre & cacher les fables proprement,*
> *Et à bien desguiser la verité des choses*
> *D'un fabuleux manteau dont elles sont encloses.*
> *J'appris en son escole à immortaliser*
> *Les hommes que je veux celebrer & priser.*

This mythological adulation reduced itself to the absurd in a poem by Marot that glorifies Francis I as what might be called *in quinis Caesar* (a synthesis of Minerva, Mars, Diana, Cupid, and Mercury) and, even more so, in a picture by Niccolò da Modena (not Niccolò dell'Abbate) illustrating this conceit. In this picture, preserved in the Cabinet des Estampes at Paris, the king is transformed into a monstrous hybrid, his bearded and behelmeted head placed on a feminine body, his breast protected by the aegis, and his feet equipped with wings. On his back he carries Diana's quiver and hunting horn; with his right arm (encased in armor while his left arm is bare) he brandishes Minerva's sword, and in his left hand he carries Mercury's caduceus and Cupid's bow. See *L'Europe humaniste; Exposition organisée par le Ministère de l'Instruction Publique, Palais des Beaux-Arts, Bruxelles, 15 décembre 1954–28 février 1955,* No. 50, Plate 49.

And when Henry II entered Paris in 1549, the role of Paris was played by Pandora. The triumphal arch erected for the occasion exhibited in its very center a figure portraying Lutetia in the guise of "La nouvelle Pandore vestue

28. AFTER JEAN COUSIN: *Triumphal Arch of Henry II*

en nymphe," who, for the benefit of His Majesty and in obvious contrast to the real Pandora (whom du Bellay was to liken to beautiful and sinful Rome), released nothing but good from a *vase antique:* she was shown "kneeling, with admirable graciousness, on a pillow as if to do homage to the king at his reception; and with one hand she pretended to open a vase of classical shape filled exclusively with all the fortunate gifts of the heavenly powers,

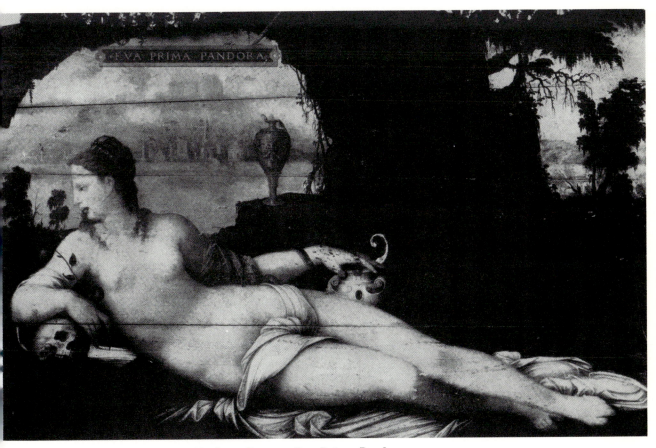

29. JEAN COUSIN: *Eva Prima Pandora*

and with no unfortunate ones." The other hand she raised as if to invite His Majesty to look up at a golden inscription saying:

> *Jadis chacun des Dieux fait un double present*
> *A la fille Vulcan qui s'en nomma Pandore.*
> *Mais, Sire, chacun d'eulx de tous biens me decore*
> *Et puis qu'à vous je suis, tout est votre a présent.*

And above this enticing figure was a simulated relief on which was painted LUTETIA NOVA PANDORA.[10]

We happen to know that the artist entrusted with the execution of this triumphal arch (*fig. 28*) was Jean Cousin.[11] And at about the same time—certainly not, as has been suggested, before 1538—the same Jean Cousin produced a famous and enigmatical picture, now in the Louvre (*fig. 29*), in which an analogous subject is treated.[12] It shows a beautiful nude reclining in front of shrubs, trees, and ruined masonry, which, forming a kind of arch, disclose the prospect of a river and an ancient city; and a tablet suspended across this arch bears the inscription: EVA PRIMA PANDORA.

The posture of this figure is patterned after that of Cellini's *Nymph of Fontainebleau,* now also in the Louvre (*fig. 30*), so much so that it has justifiably been called a "transposition en peinture" of this famous relief.[13] The city in the background, however, boasting a pyramid and a spiralized column, evokes the memory of Rome. This lends great probability to a hypothesis, advanced by Maurice Roy,[14] according to which an iconographical connection may exist between the *Eva Prima Pandora* in the Louvre and the *Lutetia Nova Pandora* in the triumphal arch of 1549, and it is even possible, we think, to

---

[10] *C'est l'Ordre qui a este tenu a la nouvelle . . . entree que . . . le Roy . . . Henry deuxsieme . . . a faicte en sa bonne ville . . . de Paris . . . ,* Paris (Boffet), 1549, especially p. 13.

[11] See M. Roy, *Artistes et monuments de la Renaissance en France,* Paris, 1929, I, p. 185.

[12] For Cousin's *Eva Prima Pandora,* see the excellent discussion in Roy, *ibidem,* pp. 56 ff., 81 ff.

[13] P. du Colombier, *L'Art Renaissance en France,* Paris, 1945, p. 86, fig. 116. Since we know by Cellini's own testimony that the *Nymph* was executed between 1541 and 1543, the latter year is the *terminus post quem* for Cousin's *Eva Prima Pandora,* and this agrees with the purely stylistic evidence, which suggests a date of toward 1550. The assumption that the picture was "probably executed in Sens before 1538" (A. Blunt, *Art and Architecture in France, 1500–1700,* Pelican History of Art, Baltimore, 1954, p. 67, Plate 46A, rec-ognizing Rosso's but not Cellini's influence) seems to rest on three facts: first, that Cousin moved from Sens to Paris about 1538; second, that the Louvre painting was in Sens ownership from at least the middle of the seventeenth century; third, that, as early as 1567, Guillaume Sotan, canon of Sens Cathedral, caused it to be repeated, with the nude Pandora transformed into a decorously attired Saint Magdalene, in a relief originally placed in the Cathedral itself and now preserved in St.-Maurice (illustrated in Roy, *op. cit.,* p. 57). However, even if it were certain that this relief was executed on the basis of the picture itself rather than a drawing and that, therefore, the picture was in Sens in or shortly before 1567, it would not follow that it was produced there before Cousin's departure for Paris; he may have sold or given it to an inhabitant of his home town at any time between *c.* 1550 and 1567.

[14] Roy, *ibidem,* p. 185 f.

restate this hypothesis in more precise and circumstantial fashion. In view of the distinctly Romelike city prospect in the Louvre picture—and, even more important, on the evidence of du Bellay's sonnet—we may assume that the woman represented in the painting was originally intended to be a *Roma* Prima Pandora rather than an *Eva* Prima Pandora. The original plan for the

30. BENVENUTO CELLINI: *Nymph of Fontainebleau*

triumphal arch would seem to have envisaged, not a single kneeling figure centrally placed between the columns, but an antithetical pair of reclining figures—one personating Paris in the guise of the "new Pandora," the other Rome in the guise of the "old Pandora"—symmetrically placed on the pediment; such pairs of reclining nymphs can be seen in countless Italian decorations as well as, to adduce a more germane example, on Jean Goujon's Fontaine des Innocents.

When the idea of such an antithetical juxtaposition was given up, Cousin, we may presume, decided to save the very attractive design originally intended for the reclining figures and to carry it out as a painting; but since a *Roma* Prima Pandora made sense only as the counterpart of a *Lutetia* Nova Pandora, he preferred to change the subject in favor of an *Eva* Prima Pandora that could stand by itself.[15] In doing so he lent visual expression to that patristic comparison which, like so much else about Pandora, had fallen into oblivion during the Middle Ages but re-emerged when the Renaissance revived Origen as well as Hesiod.[16] No one needs to be told that the parallel between Pandora and Eve was a favorite motif of Milton's,[17] and the popularity it had gained during the sixteenth century can be gauged by the fact that Carel van Mander, writing before 1603, thought it necessary explicitly to disassociate himself from what he considered an improper fusion of the sacred and the profane. "Whether the wise and learned Greeks," he writes in accordance with a fundamental tenet of both the Counter Reformation and Protestantism, "intended the story of Pandora to indicate that the first woman was the cause of all human misery, this I leave to everyone's discretion. I have no wish or intention to mix sacred, pure Scripture with vulgar, heathen tales. Some, to be sure, do interpret it [viz., the story] as referring to EVE; but I say that the creation of Pandora by Vulcan means only that heat and the just temper of the air make for a fruitful and opulent year."[18] As for France, an elaborate comparison between the stories of Pandora and the Fall of Man is found in the *Conformité des merveilles anciennes avec les modernes*, by Henri Estienne, who proves their analogy "en prenant le premier homme

---

[15] The pictures by Jan Massys showing reclining nudes in front of a city prospect, such as the Stockholm *Flora* with its view of Genoa (S. Strömbom, *Nationalmusei Mästerverk*, E. Wettergren, pref., Stockholm, 1949, p. 56, No. 12), would seem to derive from the same tradition as does Cousin's *Eva Prima Pandora*.

[16] See E. Wind, "The Revival of Origen," *Studies in Art and Literature for Belle da Costa Greene*, Princeton, 1954, pp. 412 ff.

[17] See below, p. 71.

[18] Carel van Mander, *Het Schilder-Boeck*, Haarlem and Alkmaar, 1604, fol. 3 (a passage kindly brought to our attention by Professor J. G. van Gelder). As the Council of Trent, while not objecting to the printing and reading of undiluted classical poetry, condemned "allegorical and tropological commentaries upon Ovid's *Metamorphoses*" (F. H. Reusch, *Die Indices Librorum Prohibitorum des sechszehnten Jahrhunderts*, Tübingen, 1886, p. 275), so did Luther reject allegories of this kind as a species of fornication (*Luthers Werke, kritische Gesamtausgabe*, XLIII, Weimar, 1912, p. 668). The rather banal interpretation adopted by van Mander himself comes, of course, from Natale Conti, *op. cit.*, IV, 6, p. 323: "Dicitur formasse Pandoram Vulcanus, quia calor & temperies apta coeli donet fertilitatem . . ."

31. Putto Reclining on a Death's Head
German woodcut

forgé par Prometheus, pour Adam: & ceste ieune fille, nommee Pandore, pour Eue: (laquelle amenee à Adam, fut cause de son mal) : & en interpretant que ce feu desrobbé du ciel, par le moyen duquel les hommes vindrent à la congnoissance des arts mechaniques, soit le fruict donnant à Adam & Eue congnoissance du bien & mal." [19]

In order to stress the theological connotations implied by the change of the subject, Cousin added the serpent that curls around the left arm of his Eva-Pandora. In addition, however, he borrowed a significant motif from an anonymous German woodcut that illustrates the then fashionable theme of "The *Putto* with the Death's Head" [20] but differs from other representations

[19] Henri Estienne, *L'Introduction au Traité de la conformité des merveilles anciennes avec les modernes*, Paris, 1566, pp. 5 ff. (kindly brought to our attention by Professor E. E. Lowinsky). It should be noted that, in the summary of the legend preceding the passage cited in our text, Pandora's vessel is described, with the accuracy befitting as great a philologist as Henri Estienne, as a *vaisseau* and not as a *boîte*.

[20] See H. W. Janson, "The Putto with a Death's Head," *Art Bulletin*, XIX, 1937, pp. 423 ff.

of this kind in that it shows the *putto* reclining and set out against a landscape with a cluster of buildings in the center (*fig. 31*). Just like this *putto*, Cousin's Cellinian nude rests her arm on a skull while in her hand she holds a branch

32. GIULIO BONASONE: *Miseria honorata*

of the fateful tree. In an obvious recollection of *Iliad,* XXIV—demonstrably known to him (see *fig. 25*)[21]—Cousin provided her with two vases rather than one. But, true to her nature, she closes the "vase of good" with her left hand while having opened the "vase of evil"; its lid is conspicuously thrown back and permits a cloud of evil spirits to escape.

[21] See above, n. 23, p. 49.

Du Bellay's "Rome-Pandore" is ambivalent; Cousin's *Lutetia Nova Pandora* has decided to "depart from evil and do good" in order to please the king; his *Eva Prima Pandora* is unmitigatedly sinful. And in an engraving by Giulio Bonasone (*fig. 32*), illustrating a humorous emblem in Achille Bocchi's *Symbolicae Quaestiones* and showing one of the few Italian Pandoras that have come to our knowledge, she appears as an impassive symbol of evil. High up in the clouds, unconcerned with what happens on earth, she reclines, like a water nymph upon her urn, upon what would be a perfectly good classical krater if we could be sure that the handles are only concealed and not absent; and from this "vaso di Pandora" (the Italians, it will be remembered, never accepted the "box" even as a figure of speech) there pour forth death and destruction without her active participation. Two devils and six snakes, having escaped from it, are about to attack a diminutive and frightened Epimetheus, who, by the presence of a gigantic statue of Rome (again!), is characterized as the classical ancestor of the addressee of the emblem. He is Marcantonio Flaminio, a well-known humanist and elegant Latin poet who, born at Serravalle, had gone to Rome as a boy and risen to a high office at the Curia. This office, Bocchi says in the accompanying poem, puts him in a position unenviable by virtue of its very distinction. Like Epimetheus, he is threatened by countless evils not of his making: his life, beset with all imaginable troubles from ingratitude and false friendship to daggers and poison, is nothing but an Ἔντιμος Ταλαιπωρία, a *Miseria honorata*, an "honor-covered misery." [22]

---

[22] Achille Bocchi, *op. cit.*, IV, 122, p. ccliv. The anonymous appendix to Pierio Valeriano's *Hieroglyphica* referred to in n. 15, p. 19, goes so far as to introduce Pandora (who in Gourbin's printer's mark had taken the place of a personification of hope) as what may be called a cumulative personification of misfortune: "Pandora mulier pyxidem in manu habens apertam, adversam fortunam, generis obscuritatem, infelicitatem, paupertatem, infamiam, aegritudinem, spei frustrationem, humanae sortis miseriam nobis adumbrat."

VI

Pandora, "Gift of All":
Elizabethans and Jacques Callot

AT THE same time, however, the French—and soon after, the English and Netherlandish—poets and humanists remembered with redoubled interest what even the Middle Ages had not forgotten: that Pandora is the "all-gifted" or the "gift of all," the *munus omnium generale*.[1] In contrast to her interpretation as the *beau mal,* there came to the surface the unequivocally positive idea of that "perfect blend or fusion of all things" which Tertullian had not hesitated to employ as a simile of Christ.

Thus, from *c.* 1580 on, her name came to be used, as in Tertullian's *Hesiodi Pandora,* in a purely laudatory sense and even achieved, like Mae West's, the status of a common noun. John Soowthern could publish, in 1584, a little volume of collected poems as *Pandora; The Musyque of the beautie of his Mistresse Diana.*[2] The *Liber amicorum* of Jan Six, containing the contributions of many friends (among them two remarkable drawings by Rembrandt), could be inscribed "Pandora, 1651."[3] And a collection of treatises

[1] See above, p. 9.

[2] Facsimile edition by G. B. Parks, New York, 1938.

[3] For the album of Jan Six, still preserved in the Six Stichting at Amsterdam, see J. Six, "Iets over Rembrandt," *Oud Holland,* XI, 1893, p. 157; *idem, Haagsche Maandblad,* I, 1924, pp. 378 ff. The vellum binding of the book, which Freule Nine Six kindly permitted us to inspect, is inscribed "Pandora, 1651," and an explanation is furnished by two loose leaves at the beginning, apparently placed there by the original owner, viz., a gouache copy after the central figure in Bloemaert's engraving (our *fig. 36*) and a small slip of paper referring thereto: "Les Dieux enrichissent PANDORE de leurs dons precieux pour la rendre agreable aux Hommes." The Six Stichting also

on alchemy could be entitled *Pandora, That Is the Most Noble Gift of God, or the Worthy and Healing Stone of the Wise Men*." [4] In his funeral eulogy on James I, John Williams, Bishop of Lincoln, says of his hero (whom he, like many of his contemporaries, identified with Solomon): "For being praesented by God himselfe with a *Pandora* of royall *graces* . . . yet tooke he out nothing but *Wisedome* to gouerne his people." [5] And an analogous, though even more exalted, simile had been used by Spenser when he addressed Queen Elizabeth as "the true *Pandora* of all heauenly graces." [6]

In all these cases the name of the mythological character is used as a generic and impersonal term, and in a soberer mood the Bishop of Lincoln and Spenser might have spoken of a "treasure house" or "cornucopia" of graces. But we learn from Thomas Dekker that the "Divine Elisa" had no objection to being addressed as "Pandora" also in the original, specific, and personal sense of the word: "Some call her Pandora: some Gloriana: some Cynthia: some Astraea: all by several names to express several loves: yet all those names make but one celestial body." [7] And that the Queen had no reason to resent this metonymy is not surprising when John Fisher could write "To frame the like Pandore, / The gods repine, and nature would grow poor," [8] and when Thomas Kyd could present her as Diana's rival even in

---

owns a "groote Pandora," a general collection of quotations, proverbs, maxims, jokes, etc., compiled by Jan Six himself in his later years. Thrifty as he was, he employed for this purpose the unused sheets in an enormous book of Town Council records, which he turned back to front and upside down; the inscription "Pandora" thus appears on what had been the back cover, whereas the original front cover is inscribed "Vroet-Schap 1679."
[4] This is, in translation, the title of the first edition of a work edited by a physician named Hieronymus Reusner: *Pandora; das ist Die edelste Gab Gottes oder der werde vnnd heilsame Stein der Weisen* . . . , Basel, 1582. A second edition of 1590, also printed at Basel, is described in *A Hundred Alchemical Books, Science Museum, London Book Exhibition*, I,

Catalogue 1952. Cf. also Martin Delrio, *Disquisitionum magicarum libri sex*, Mainz, 1612, p. 59: ". . . Pandorae poculum [*sic*] hoc [*scil.*, the philosopher's stone] esse contendunt ab Hesiodo notatum." For Ben Jonson's use of this passage as well as others from the same source, see above, n. 13, p. 19.
[5] John [Williams], Bishop of Lincoln, *Great Britains Salomon*, London, 1625, pp. 14 f. The passage was kindly brought to our attention by Professor Warren Todd Furniss.
[6] Spenser, *Teares of the Muses*, 577 ff.; Smith and de Selincourt, *op. cit.*, p. 486.
[7] Thomas Dekker, *Old Fortunatus*, quoted in F. A. Yates, "Queen Elizabeth as Astraea," *Journal of the Warburg and Courtauld Institutes*, X, 1947, p. 27.
[8] John Fisher, *Fuimus Troes*, quoted in *The Oxford English Dictionary*, s.v. "Pandora."

chastity: "Was she not chaste?—As is Pandora or Dianaes thoughts." [9] A climax was reached, about half a century later, when an engraved portrait of Christina of Sweden was inscribed with the following verses:

> *O quam te memorem, virgo! Quam tanta Venustas,*
> *Ingenium, Eloquium, Doctrina, Potentia, Virtus*
> *Certatim exornant; poteras Pandora videri,*
> *Ni Christina fores, melioribus inclyta donis,*
> *Exitio nec ficta hominum, sed facta saluti.*

("How shall I name thee, Virgin, whom such Beauty,/Genius, Speech, and Learning, Might and Virtue/Vie to adorn? Thou might'st be called Pandora/Wert thou not, famed for better gifts, Christina—/Born for man's bliss, not molded for his ruin.") [10]

True, neither the eulogist of Queen Christina nor Spenser, the translator of du Bellay's *Antiquitez de Rome*, could entirely forget the sinister implications of the Hesiodian story, and when Spenser evoked the image of Pandora in a private love poem, he conceived this image after the time-honored pattern of the *beau mal:*

> *When I behold that beauties wonderment,*
> *And rare perfection of each goodly part:*
> *of natures skill the onely complement,*
> *I honor and admire the makers art.*
> *But when I feele the bitter balefull smart,*
> *which her fayre eyes vnwares doe worke in mee:*
> *that death out of theyr shiny beames doe dart,*
> *I thinke that I a new Pandora see;*
> *Whom all the Gods in councell did agree,*
> *into this sinfull world from heauen to send:*
> *that she to wicked men a scourge should bee,*

---

[9] Thomas Kyd, *Soliman and Perseda*, 2131 f.
[10] These lines, brought to our attention by Dr. Carl Nordenfalk, form the legend of David van den Bremden's engraving after a portrait of Queen Christina by David Beck, dated 1649; see K. E. Steneberg, *Kristinatidens Målari*, Malmö, 1955, Plate 28.

> *For all their faults with which they did offend.*
> *But since ye are my scourge I will intreat,*
> *that for my faults ye will me gently beat.*[11]

But even here the responsibility for Pandora's disastrous action is significantly shifted to the offenses of "wicked men," so that she becomes an instrument of divine retribution rather than an evil force per se; and a similarly forgiving attitude can be detected in Milton's world-renowned description of the First Marriage:

> *. . . Here in close recess*
> *With Flowers, Garlands, and sweet-smelling Herbs*
> *Espoused Eve deckt first her Nuptial Bed,*
> *And heav'nly Quires the Hymenaean sung*
> *What day the genial Angel to our Sire*
> *Brought her in naked beauty more adorn'd*
> *More lovely than Pandora, whom the Gods*
> *Endowd with all their gifts and O too like*
> *In sad event, when to the unwiser Son*
> *Of Japhet brought by Hermes, she ensnar'd*
> *Mankind with her faire looks, to be aveng'd*
> *On him who had stole Jove's authentic fire.*[12]

In art a representation of that collective effort of the Olympians to which Pandora owed her superhuman perfection,[13] the *Pandoras genesis* glorified by Phidias, did not reappear until Callot produced the etching called *La Création de Pandore (fig. 33).*[14] This etching is divided into two zones, and the heroine appears twice, before and after her descent to earth. In the upper zone Pandora, entirely nude, stands on a cloud in a beautiful, resilient pose, while all the gods are grouped around her. Placed directly beneath

---

[11] Spenser, *Amoretti,* xxiv; Smith and de Selincourt, *op. cit.,* p. 566.
[12] Milton, *Paradise Lost,* IV, 708 ff. In the *Doctrine and Discipline of Divorce,* II, 3 (quoted in *The Oxford English Dictionary, s.v.* "Pandora"), Milton compares Eve to Pandora in

terms even more flattering to both: "The Academics and Stoics, who knew what a consummat and most adorned Pandora was bestow'd upon Adam . . ."
[13] Cf. above, p. 9.
[14] J. Lieure, *Jacques Callot,* II *(Catalogue),* 2, Paris, 1925, p. 65, No. 568.

the eagle-borne Jupiter (and with Vulcan proudly pointing to his master-piece), she raises the portentous vase in a gesture of triumph; but in the upper left-hand corner Death can be seen pursuing a victim. In the lower zone Pandora has alighted in a luminous landscape, and, while her beauty remains as radiant as it had been in heaven, her deportment has changed. She is no longer entirely nude; her posture is demure rather than self-confident; and instead of raising the vessel aloft, she holds it at eye level and seems to look at it as if in doubt whether she should open it. On the left a solitary figure withdraws as if in fear; he may be Epimetheus, still mindful of his brother's warnings.

Universal though Callot's interests were in every other respect, they did not extend to classical mythology. His *Pandora* is the one and only exception. And since it represents a subject very novel at the time, it may be presumed to have been executed with a special purpose in mind. The print is unanimously dated about 1625, two or three years after Callot's return from Florence to his native Lorraine, and it was in this very year, 1625, that his sovereign, Duke Charles IV, married Nicole, Duchesse de Bar, a little cousin only seventeen years of age. Callot dedicated to her his famous *Parterre de Nancy*.[15] Given the fact that the period did not hesitate to compare Pandora to a great lady—even, as we have seen, to Queen Elizabeth—one might be tempted to surmise that Callot's print was inspired by the advent of the young Duchess and was meant to express admiration and hope as well as wistful doubt as to her future development.

There is, however, another and, in our opinion, preferable interpretation. Quite shortly after her marriage Nicole fell from grace, and by the end of 1626 there appeared at Nancy, exiled from Paris by Cardinal Richelieu, Marie de Rohan, Duchesse de Chevreuse. Well favored, full of *esprit*, not overly virtuous, and one of the greatest schemers in history, she completely conquered the inflammable heart and mind of the Duke. And as Callot had dedicated the *Parterre de Nancy* to Nicole, so did he immortalize, less than

---

[15] Lieure, *ibidem*, p. 64, No. 566.

33. JACQUES CALLOT: *Creation and Descent of Pandora*

two years later, the *Combat de la Barrière* held on February 14, 1627, in honor of the Duchesse de Chevreuse. The dedicatory poem of this print contains such verses as:

> *Princesse, en ces graces parfaite*
> *De qui les Cieux vous ont orné*
> *Le iour de France est borné*
> *Ne pouuant estre qu'où vous êtes.*[16]

This highborn adventuress, "adorned with perfect charms by the heavens" but disastrous for the country and the Duke, whom she involved in countless financial and political difficulties, would seem to be a more likely

---

[16] Lieure, *ibidem*, p. 71, Nos. 575–588.

object of Callot's mythological allusion than the innocent, luckless Nicole. And this assumption is borne out, not only by the presence of such distinctly negative symbols as Death and the reluctant Epimetheus, but also by the

34. Jacques Callot: *Luxury*

fact that Callot's "terrestrial" Pandora repeats in nearly every detail a beautiful figure that he had designed, some six or seven years before, as a personification of Luxury (*fig. 34*).[17]

It is interesting to compare Callot's *Pandore* with one of the illustrations in Michel de Marolles' *Tableaux du temple des Muses tirez du cabinet de feu M. Favereau*, published in Paris in 1655: an engraving by Cornelis Bloemaert (*fig. 36*)[18] after a drawing, preserved in the Städelsches Kunstinstitut

---

[17] Lieure, *ibidem*, p. 13, No. 357.
[18] Professor Julius S. Held kindly informs us that all the plates for de Marolles' book were finished in 1638, which year thus constitutes a *terminus ante quem* for van Diepenbeeck's drawing. A new edition of the work, published in 1733, was illustrated with literal copies of the Bloemaert engravings by Bernard Picart, which are inscribed with legends in four languages and printed in four different styles of types: *La Boëte de Pandore* in roman capitals, *Pandora's Box* in upper- and lower-case italics,

at Frankfurt, by Abraham van Diepenbeeck (*fig. 35*).[19] Van Diepenbeeck's drawing is essentially a free variation of the upper section of Callot's print;

35. ABRAHAM VAN DIEPENBEECK: *Creation of Pandora*

but at his hands Pandora is completely de-demonized, and it is perhaps for precisely this reason that his elegantly academic composition achieved far

Die Büchse der Pandora in *Fraktur*, and *De Doos van Pandora* in upper- and lower-case roman. The same scene was floridly represented by Pierre Mignard in a fresco in Versailles, unfortunately destroyed in 1736 (a circumstantial description, partly quoted in Larousse, *loc. cit.*, is found in Piganiol de la Force, *op. cit.*, I, pp. 313 ff.); and, in an abbreviated version, in another French composition of the seventeenth century that, in 1926,

was in the possession of Mr. J. Hogeraats. Submitted to the Rijksbureau voor Kunsthistorische Documentatie at The Hague but apparently not photographed, it showed Pandora adorned by nymphs while Neptune emerged in the foreground and a palace was seen on the right.

[19] Van Diepenbeeck's drawing is here reproduced after a photograph kindly supplied by the Rijksbureau voor Kunsthistorische Documentatie (No. L.6663).

36. Cornelis Bloemaert after Abraham van Diepenbeeck: *Creation of Pandora*

greater popularity than its superior model. By its very nature and its very history the Pandora theme was not conducive to the formation of recognized and fairly constant "types"; the artists, basing their inventions upon the written or spoken word rather than a visual experience, seem to make a fresh start in each case. Callot's composition, which did exert some influence on later generations, is the only exception; but it was only through the intermediary of van Diepenbeeck's adaptation—or, rather, Bloemaert's engraving after it, a partial copy of which was, characteristically, enclosed in Jan Six's *Liber amicorum*, just mentioned—that it could give rise to something like a "representational tradition." [20]

The very fact that van Diepenbeeck limited the theme to the event in heaven, thus emphasizing Pandora's celestial essence rather than her terrestrial activities, serves to present her in a favorable light, and he changed every detail so as to neutralize her dangerous qualities: she is no longer the triumphant καλὸν κακόν, raising her vase like a symbol of victory and arousing the amazed admiration of the very Olympians. Rather she is a timid maiden overwhelmed by what is happening to her and using the fateful pyxis as a fig leaf—a motif charmingly, if somewhat whimsically, commented upon by de Marolles.[21] The fearsome image of Death is absent. Jupiter, instead of dominating the scene as a prime mover of evil, borne down from on high and brandishing his thunderbolt, is relegated to a corner whence he and Juno, a

---

[20] See below, p. 107.

[21] M. de Marolles, *op. cit.*, p. 36: "Il semble que l'Auteur de ces Peintures ne l'a point representée sans sujet tenant sa boëte de la main droite, baissée vers la partie qu'elle couure, d'où se sont écoulées tant de misères et d'inquiétudes entre les hommes, comme s'il vouloit dire que du milieu de la fontaine des délices s'eleue tousiours quelque amertume, & quelque chose qui pique parmy les fleurs." De Marolles' text is interesting also in several other respects. He not only specifies and explains the gift of each god, but also refers to the crucial passage in Erasmus' *Adagia* (translating the proverb into "Le fol devient sage par le mal qu'il a receu"); and though he captions

Bloemaert's engraving with three lines from Hesiod, he not only accepts the Philodemian version seemingly championed by Erasmus, but improves upon it, so to speak, by asserting that Jupiter had first prepared the box, filled with all evils, and subsequently ordered Vulcan to create Pandora as a bait the tastiness of which would induce Epimetheus to accept the gift: "Jupiter, après luy auoir mis entre les mains la boëte dans laquelle il auoit enferme tous les maux, l'envoya vers Epiméthée, homme de peu de sens, qui la receut pour sa femme auec le present qu'elle apportoit, dont il ne se defioit point; mes dès le moment que la sotte curiosité luy eut fait ouurir la boëte, les maux sortirent en foule pour se disperser par toute la terre."

contented married couple, look at Pandora with the same cheerful satisfaction as do the lesser gods; and the place of honor in the upper center is reserved for five of the Muses, who, naturally, had no place in Callot's print.

37. Sébastien Le Clerc: *Epimetheus Opening Pandora's Box*

VII

Πιθοιγία:
Hesiod *vs.* Babrius *et al.*

IT MIGHT be expected that the dramatic climax of the Pandora story, the actual opening of the vessel, would become a favorite subject of Renaissance and Baroque art; but such is not the case. Rosso's magnificent composition remained without following, except for those three printer's marks where the principal figure is changed from an agent of disaster to a personification of hope. And of the three other sixteenth- and seventeenth-century representations of the actual πιθοιγία that have come to our attention, none adheres to the orthodox, Hesiodian version of the myth.

One of these three, Sébastien Le Clerc's amusing engraving in Isaac de Benserade's *Ovide en rondeaux* of 1676 (*fig. 37*),[1] follows the Philodemian

---

[1] Le Clerc's engraving, found on p. 10 of Isaac de Benserade's *Metamorphoses d'Ovide en rondeaux*, is mentioned but not illustrated in M. D. Henkel, "Illustrierte Ausgaben von Ovids Metamorphosen im XV., XVI. und XVII. Jahrhundert," *Vorträge der Bibliothek Warburg*, 1926 / 1927, p. 137. The legend says: "La complaisance de Pandore pour un de ses Amans fut cause qu'elle luy laissa ouvrir une Boëste que les Dieux luy avoient mise entre les mains, d'où il se répandit un nombre infini de misères. Cette Fable n'est point de la Metamorphose, mais elle est trop celebre pour n'y estre pas inséree." And the accompanying, slightly suggestive *Rondeau* reads as follows:

Dans une Boëste un trésor odieux
Fut renfermé par le vouloir des Dieux.
Pandore en fut seule dépositaire,
Ce n'estoit pas une Beauté vulgaire,
Le premiers coeurs céderent à ses yeux.
Ayant en main ce Bijoux precieux,
Elle s'alla promener en tous lieux;
Quand on est belle, on ne demeure guère
Dans une Boëste.
Quelqu'un luy plût; ce quelqu'un curieux
Ouvrit en fin ce qu'elle aimoit le mieux,
Il n'en sortit que peine & que misère
Dont les humains, hélas! n'avoient que faire,
Et ce fut là ce qui nous vint des cieux,
Dans une Boëste.

variant, apparently sanctioned by Erasmus of Rotterdam, according to which the fatal vessel was not opened by a naughty Pandora but by a "stupidly curious" Epimetheus; [2] and its text adds to Pandora's traditional charms and shortcomings an engaging inability to say "no." Instead of being Pandora's husband, Epimetheus has become "un de ses Amans," and it is her complaisance toward him which "fut cause qu'elle luy laissa ouvrir une Boëste que les Dieux luy avoient mis entre les mains, d'où il se répandit un nombre infini de misères."

To this very French interpretation of the Pandora story, staged in a richly appointed boudoir, the second rendering of the πιθοιγία, Pieter Serwouters' engraving (*fig. 38*) briefly referred to above,[3] opposes that sober, homespun realism which, as demonstrated in a brilliant lecture by J. G. van Gelder, distinguishes a Dutch emblem book such as Roemer Visscher's *Sinnepoppen* from its Italian, French, and even Flemish parallels.[4] Serwouters,

---

"Pandore ouvrant la boîte fatale" was also represented by Charles Le Brun in the house of his friend, the great architect François Mansart, but has disappeared together with the house itself (Larousse, *loc. cit.*); it is a pity that we cannot compare this work with the nearly contemporaneous *frivolité* of Le Clerc. Neither have we been able to locate a probably not-too-exciting painting by Jean Alaux, showing "Pandore ouvrant la boîte fatale," which was exhibited at the Paris Salon of 1824 (Larousse, *loc. cit.*).

[2] An Italian poem adhering to the Philodemus-Erasmus version was pointed out to us by Professor E. E. Lowinsky: G. B. Giraldi Cinthio, *Dell'Hercole*, Modena, 1557, pp. 283 f. (Canto XXI):

> *Et s'Epimeteo, suo sciocco fratello*
> *Lasciava chiuso il vaso di Pandora,*
> *L'huomo si lunge era da caso fello,*
> *C'havuta non havria infelice un'hora,*
> *Ma che semplicemente il miserello*
> *Laperse e'incontinente usciro fora*
> *I mali, ch'ove prima eran contenti*
> *Gli huomini, esser gli fer tristi, & dolenti.*

[3] See p. 52, the text translated in n. 28. In a poem by Jan Vos, brought to our attention by

Professor J. G. van Gelder, the then entirely proverbial Pandora's box is playfully contrasted with a little amber box presented to a Dutch lady by the Elector of Brandenburg:

> *Pandoora plag weleer te brallen met haar*
> *   doos.*
> *Maar toen sy 't slot ontsloot, o helsche gru-*
> *   wlykheeden!*
> *Verscheen de tieranny, en al wat goddeloos*
> *Genoemt wordt, onder 't volk, om 't aardtryk*
> *   te bestryen.*

(Jan Vos, *Alle de Gedichten*, Amsterdam, I, 1662, p. 222). In free translation the verses read: "Pandora used to boast about her box; but when she opened the lock—oh, hellish horrors—tyranny spread among mankind and all that which we call godless came to sway the earth. But whoever will unseal *this* secret receptacle [viz., the little amber box]. . . ."

[4] Professor van Gelder's lecture was delivered at the Institute of Fine Arts of New York University and will, we hope, be published in the not-too-distant future. Roemer Visscher's *Sinnepoppen*, Amsterdam, 1614, is now available in a facsimile edition prefaced by L. Brummer, The Hague, 1949.

Hier Maya: blye-Zoon Pandora leyd' te trouwen
tot Epimetheus heen die vlytigh om te schouwen
haar Bruyd-gaaf vande Goon, de gulde doos op doet
daar In besloten was van Iupiter het goet
en t Quaat al onder een: op dat den Mensch geen klaagen
Zoo weeld' hem houden cost en hadd van al syn daagen:
maar ach hier vlieght het heen de deughden na de lucht
en d'ondeucht hier omleegh: daar noch den Mensch om sucht
Dees Zotte Vrouws bedryf most Epimeth' becoopen
Die nu voor al zyn heyl hout maar Alleen de Hoope

38. PIETER SERWOUTERS:
Pandora Brought to Epimetheus by Mercury

locating the event at the door of an unpretentious Dutch house, follows the orthodox version in that the opening of the *doos* is left to Pandora. Abnormal and significant, however, is, we recall, the fact—stressed in the accompanying poem—that Jupiter has filled the box with good as well as evil in order to ensure a balanced state of affairs. When the lid is lifted, the Virtues (*deughden*) escape into the air so as to be lost to mankind while Vice (*ondeucht*) spreads all over the earth.

The notion that the vessel contains a blend of good and evil rather than either the one or the other exclusively derives, as has been seen, from Homer. But the idea that the Virtues fly into the air, leaving the earth behind them, is an obvious reminiscence of Babrius, who makes them flee "heavenwards from the earth." [5] And this brings us to the third and most puzzling of the πιθοιγίαι here to be considered: a quite impressive engraving by Giulio Bonasone, the illustrator of Bocchi's *Symbolicae Quaestiones* (*fig. 39*). It has been described by Bartsch—so far as we know, the only author to mention it—as "Epiméthée ouvrant la boîte fatale de Pandore d'où sortent toutes les vertus qui s'envolent au ciel, n'y laissant que l'espérance." [6] However, while Bonasone's print does show the vessel opened by a man rather than a woman and discharging Virtues rather than Vices, it fails to correspond to Bartsch's description in every other respect.

There is no reference whatever to Pandora, nor is there any evidence to show that the leading character is Epimetheus; in an engraving teeming with inscriptions he is, on the contrary, the only anonymous figure. In reality, Bonasone's engraving is an elaborate and faithful illustration of the Babrius fable, which, we remember, limits the content of the pithos to goods and, omitting all proper names, makes no individual person but "man" as such,

---

[5] See above, p. 8, and n. 13, *ibidem*. The influence of Babrius' *Fables*—perhaps just because they were read by young people—must have been much stronger in the old days than might be expected. In his *Vers lyriques* (see above, pp. 52 f.), even Joachim du Bellay, certainly familiar with Hesiod and one of the earliest, if not the earliest, writers to use "la boête de Pandore" as a proverbial phrase (Preface to *Deux Livres de l'Enéide de Virgile* of 1552, Chamard, *op. cit.*, vi, 1931, p. 248), makes Virtues rather than Vices escape from Pandora's box.

[6] Bartsch, *Le Peintre Graveur*, xv, p. 149, No. 144.

39. Giulio Bonasone: *"Man" Opening the Fateful Vessel*

ἄνθρωπος, the hero of the tragedy.[7] In perfect accordance with this version, the act is performed by a figure representing the species *Homo sapiens* in terms as typical as possible: a bearded man of middle age distinguished only by his "eagerness to know," his anonymity stressed by the fact that every one of the other figures is identified not only by attributes but also in writing. The escaping goods are carefully labeled *Virtus* (Virtue in general, appropriately represented as a diminutive Minerva), *Fortitudo, Laetitia, Libertas, Felicitas, Pax, Clementia, Aequitas, Concordia,* and *Salus;* even the unmistakable figure of Hope, attempting to crawl out of the big vessel but about to be caught by the lid, is inscribed *Spes.*

Some special attention should be paid to the vessel itself. Far from being a *boîte*, it is a big vase, and not only a vase *generaliter sumptum* but a remarkably authentic-looking if somewhat elephantine stamnos, the attachments of its handles imitating metal technique, as is so often the case with genuine classical specimens.[8] We are faced, then, with a definite attempt to represent the pithos in what may be called an antiquarian spirit, the only comparable instance being the *Miseria honorata* emblem (*fig. 32*), where, we recall, the "vaso di Pandora" appears in the guise of a less accurately rendered yet clearly recognizable krater.

It is perhaps more than an accident that this *Miseria honorata* is also a work of Bonasone's, and that both he and his patron, Achille Bocchi, lived in Bologna. An artist active in this learned university town, the *fons et origo* of all emblem books, could easily learn that a Greek pithos was a large clay vessel, though he and his advisers were probably ignorant of its specific characteristics. And in an attempt to make it "genuine" as well as big he imitated, not without success, whatever other specimens of large-scale ancient pottery were within his reach.

---

[7] See, again, above, p. 8.

[8] For the technical definition of a stamnos ("high-shouldered, short-necked jar with two handles set horizontally"), see G. M. A. Richter and M. J. Milne, *Shapes and Names of Athenian Vases*, New York, 1935, pp. 8 f., figs. 64–68; we follow their terminology also with respect to other types of Greek vases. For a less scientific yet classical-minded transformation of the Homeric pithoi in the emblem books, see *figs. 26, 27*, and cf. n. 23, pp. 49 f.

VIII

Romanticism, Classicist and Victorian

To find another effort to break the spell of the Erasmian tradition—that is to say, to restore Pandora's "box" to its rightful size and to at least a semblance of its rightful shape—we must go down to the end of the eighteenth century. And even this second, more concerted, effort at archaeological accuracy was limited to a period and an environment in which the physical discovery of Pompeii and Herculaneum, the aesthetic discovery of "Etruscan" vases in the circle of Sir William Hamilton,[1] and the spiritual discovery of the "Hellenic soul" by Winckelmann, the Comte de Caylus, and Lessing had changed the attitude toward classical antiquity. For these events had given rise to a new kind of Classicism, which (in contrast to Poussin's, or, for that matter, Pietro da Cortona's) may be described as both Romantic and doctrinaire—Romantic in that an idea unattainable for the present tended to be mistaken for a reality believed to have existed in the past, doctrinaire in that nevertheless (or, perhaps, for this very reason) a passionate effort was made to regain this Paradise Lost by means of scientific reconstruction[2] rather than creative assimilation.

[1] With a few exceptions such as Pollaiuolo (F. Shapley, "A Student of Ancient Ceramics, Antonio Pollaiuolo," Art Bulletin, II, 1919, pp. 78 ff.) and, possibly, Francesco di Giorgio Martini, Greek vases do not seem to have exerted a considerable influence on Renaissance and seventeenth-century art. The Aretine vases so much appreciated by Ristoro d'Arezzo about 1287 are an exceptional case in that they show reliefs rather than flat designs and are fashioned of a highly polished material; their fragments could be appreciated, one may say, on the same level as classical cameos.

[2] To receive a vivid impression of this combination of emotional appropriation and scientific reconstruction, one may consider the subjects proposed, in part with explicit reference to their previous treatment by Flaxman, for the annual competitions of Goethe's Weimarer Kunstfreunde: Helen Brought to Paris by Aphrodite; Achilles among the Daughters of

It was, characteristically, in England (where the roots of such an attitude can be traced back to the very beginnings of a national civilization)[3] that this new kind of Classicism reached a maximum of vigor and pervasiveness.[4] And it was this English development which brought about the re-emergence of our heroine, the long-neglected Pandora, who—apart from a marginal appearance in François Lemoyne's ceiling of the "Salon d'Hercule" in Versailles [4a]—seems to be absent from the artistic scene between 1676, the date of de Benserade's *Ovide en rondeaux,* and about one hundred years later. She who had been an almost exclusively French figure in the sixteenth century and, during the seventeenth, had managed to cross the borders of the Netherlands [5] became a specifically Anglo-Saxon figure from the last quarter of the eighteenth.

Lycomedes; Achilles Battling the Rivers Skamandros and Simoeis; Odysseus Plying the Cyclopes with Wine; and, most characteristically, a reconstruction of Polygnotus' murals in the Lesche at Delphi (*Goethes Kunstschriften,* II, Leipzig, 1912, pp. 188 ff., 303 ff., 321 ff., 364 ff.).

[3] In 1151, Bishop Henry of Winchester bought and set up a number of Roman statues in spite of their pagan flavor, while Magister Gregory of Oxford, equally enraptured with the beauty of classical sculpture, recorded the measurements of Roman buildings (cf. M. R. James, "Magister Gregorius de Mirabilibus Urbis Romae," *English Historical Review,* XXXII, 1917, pp. 531 ff.; G. McN. Rushforth, "Magister Gregorius de Mirabilibus Urbis Romae . . . ," *Journal of Roman Studies,* IX, 1919, pp. 44 ff.; E. F. Jacob, "Some Aspects of Classical Influence in Mediaeval England," *Vorträge der Bibliothek Warburg,* X, 1930-1931, pp. 14 ff.; S. A. Larrabee, *English Bards and Grecian Marbles,* New York, 1943, pp. 20 ff.). And at the very beginning of English poetry there stands *The Ruin* (N. Kershaw, *Anglo-Saxon and Norse Poems,* Cambridge, 1922, pp. 51 ff.), where the remains of a Roman town (Bath?) destroyed by "Fate" are described in a spirit prophetic of Romanticism at its somber best.

[4] As for a parallel development in Germany, we may refer to a composition by Peter Cornelius, executed in 1820 by Clemens von Zimmermann, on the ceiling of the "Kleine

Vorhalle" in the Glyptothek at Munich. This ceiling (see A. Furtwängler, *Beschreibung der Glyptothek König Ludwigs I,* 2nd edition, P. Wolters, ed., Munich, 299; H. von Einem, "Peter Cornelius," *Wallraf-Richartz Jahrbuch,* XVI, 1954, pp. 104 ff., particularly p. 121) was intended to symbolize the glory, tragedy, and ultimate salvation of the "creative" artist. A central roundel showed the formation of man by Prometheus and his animation by Pallas Athene; a lunette on the right, Epimetheus and Pandora, the latter having opened her vessel and permitted the evils to escape; and a lunette on the left, the deliverance of the fettered Prometheus by Hercules. These three paintings were destroyed during the war without having been photographed. Peter Cornelius' original cartoon for the Epimetheus and Pandora composition is, however, preserved in the Nationalgalerie at Berlin (see H. Jordan, *Catalog der Königlichen Nationalgalerie zu Berlin,* 1901, p. 326, No. 70); and we are able, in the nick of time, to include a reproduction of it (*fig. 41a*).

[4a] See *Revue nouvelle des arts,* XIV, 1861, pp. 197 ff., particularly p. 200: "Au dessous de Pandore et Diane on voit Mars attentif à la chute des Monstres et des Vices." We owe this reference to Mr. Martin Davies.

[5] A singularly unattractive seventeenth-century painting, preserved in the Palazzo Reale at Genoa and hopefully ascribed to Rubens (Alinari photograph No. 15404), does not, however, represent Pandora. The vessel lov-

40. JAMES BARRY: *Creation of Pandora*

The series of English Pandoras opens with a cartoon sent to the Royal Academy Exhibition of 1775 by James Barry; it was elaborated into a huge canvas (120 x 204 in.; according to the artist himself, 10 x 18 ft.), which was exhibited at the Royal Academy in 1791 and is now in the City Art Gallery at Manchester (*figs. 40* and *41*).[6] This canvas, minutely described and

ingly embraced by a woman elaborately dressed after the fashion of the Venetian Renaissance is obviously a funerary urn (cf., e.g., the specimen reproduced in A. Baumeister, *Denkmäler des klassischen Altertums*, Munich and Leipzig, 1885–1888, I, p. 136, fig. 145), and the woman herself would seem to be Artemisia, the widow of Mausolos. Prior to building the famous monument named after him, she was allegedly so unable to tear herself away from his ashes that she had them ground up into a powder and drank them mixed with water and perfumes (Aulus Gellius, *Noctes Atticae*, x, 18). The same Artemisia may be the subject of the French sixteenth-century painting reproduced by de Hevesy (n. 22, p. 26), as was proposed by A. Firmin-Didot ("Miniatures de Jean Cousin," *Gazette des Beaux-Arts*, ser. 2, IV, 1870, pp. 406 ff.), and it is possible that the *Pandora* (statue by Armand Lefèvre) seen by Piganiol de la Force at Marly (*op. cit.*, II, p. 288) is in reality identical with Lefèvre's *Artemisia* at Versailles (Thieme-Becker, *Allgemeines Künstlerlexikon*, XXII, p. 550).

[6] See *The Works of James Barry, Esq., Historical Painter*, London, 1809, II, pp. 143 ff.; cf. W. T. Whitley, *Artists and Their Friends in England*, London, 1927, I, p. 143 f., II, pp. 310 f.; T. Bodkin, "James Barry, Part II . . . ," *Apollo*, XXXIII, 1941, pp. 1 ff. (with illustration on p. 4). The reference in *The Works of James Barry* was brought to our attention by Professor H. von Erffa, and we are grateful to Mr. S. D. Cleveland for kindly providing us with photographs.

41. JAMES BARRY: *Zeus*. Detail of fig. 40

eruditely commented upon by James Barry himself, shows, to use his own phrase, "Pandora in an assembly of the Gods, decorated for the accomplishment of her future destiny." But the scene as he saw it bears little resemblance to that envisaged by Callot and van Diepenbeeck (*figs. 33, 35,* and *36*).

Fully conscious of the time-honored but often forgotten parallel between Pandora and Eve (he calls her story "one of the most splendid of the many specimens of the Heathen manner of adumbrating and allegorizing that introduction of Evil or fall of mankind which is celebrated in Genesis"),[7] Barry represented the heroine as a creature still devoid of will and consciousness, reclining in an abandoned pose not unlike that of Michelangelo's Adam.[8] And, since he had shrewdly observed the analogy between the myths of Pandora and Psyche, calling his subject "almost similar to that of Raffael's where the same personages would occur,"[9] he lived up to his avowed intention to revive the frescoes on the Farnesina ceiling by assimilating his work as much as he could to them in style and figure types. On the other hand, he introduced, as he points out with justifiable pride, a number of new "conceits," such as Minerva as a teacher of painting rather than needlework and one of the Fates "coming forward holding the fatal vase in which those evils and calamities of life are concealed which Jupiter had prepared as a secret portion or dowry."[10] And, last but not least, he attempted to reshape the whole scene according to the standards of that Romantic Classicism which dominated the taste of his period. The chair on which Pandora reclines, its back gracefully curved after the fashion of the specimens in Greek steles, is decorated with an almost too-conspicuous egg-and-dart pattern, and the "fatal vessel," presented to Zeus on a platter, is a kylix enormously magnified and transposed into metal but admirably correct in shape; the modern beholder may find it somewhat difficult to imagine it closed, but should remember the fact that

---

[7] *The Works of James Barry*, p. 147.
[8] It may or may not be an accident that the as yet inanimate Pandora is described as "reclining" (*couchée*) in Voltaire's opera *Pan-*dore (cf. p. 121), an English translation of which was published in 1772.
[9] *The Works of James Barry*, p. 143.
[10] *Ibidem*, p. 153.

41a. PETER CORNELIUS: *Pandora Opening the Vase*

Barry's contemporaries were accustomed to seeing the kylix form adopted for covered dishes and soup tureens.[11]

One of the most characteristic aspects of this Romantic Classicism is that it produced, in addition to a new interpretation of forms and subjects, a new technique of visual presentation: engravings consisting of outlines without either color or modeling. Thus far, such simple contours had been employed only in preliminary sketches or, as a final vehicle of communication, for the illustration of such scientific treatises as Jean Pèlerin's *De artificiali perspectiva*, Dürer's *Vier Bücher von menschlicher Proportion*, or Leonhard Fuchs' *De historia stirpium;* now they achieved the status of an artistic medium *sui generis*. What had been a means of diagrammatic abbreviation rose to the dignity of a style.

Pure line engravings appeared, characteristically, in a great number of antiquarian publications printed in Germany and England in the last quarter

---

[11] A particularly striking instance is a lidded silver bowl in the Nationalmuseum at Stockholm (1798) that was designed by the well-known dilettante, Karl August Ehrensvärd, and executed by Simson Ryberg (*Mästerverk i Nationalmuseum, Konsthantverk*, C. Hernmarck, ed., Stockholm, 1954, pp. 148 f.).

of the eighteenth century.[12] Here the restriction of the illustrations to plain contours may originally have been promoted by didactic, in part even economic, considerations; we happen to know that Wilhelm Tischbein's *Collection of Engravings from Ancient Vases . . . in the Possession of Sir William Hamilton* (first volume, 1791) was launched because the owner wished to supplement P.-F. d'Hancarville's magnificent facsimile edition of his treasures [13] by a series of volumes that were not too expensive for scholars and young artists.[14] But it was soon realized that these chaste contour prints lent tangible expression not only to the ontological superiority accorded to the line in the theory of cognition (had not Thomas Aquinas asserted that the relation between image and prototype rests on *figura* rather than *color* because "if the color of anything is depicted on a wall, this is not called an image unless the figure is also depicted"?),[15] but also to the aesthetic superiority accorded to it in all idealistic theories of art, and to the metaphysical superiority accorded to it by every type of Platonism. Simple line drawings, Frans Hemsterhuys wrote in 1769, retain more of the "godlike fire of the first-conceived idea [*denkbeeld*] than paintings." [16] Reduced to pure contours, the visible world in general, and the precious relics of antiquity in particular, seemed to assume an unearthly, ethereal character, detached from the "material" qualities of color, weight, and surface texture; and we can easily conceive that the line engravings found in the archaeological publications of the

---

[12] The following instances may be mentioned: Georg Christoph Kilian's illustrations in C. G. Murr, *Abbildungen der Gemälde und Alterthümer welche seit 1738 . . . in der verschütteten Stadt Herkulanum . . . an das Licht gebracht worden* (first volume, 1777); Wilhelm Tischbein's *Collection of Engravings from Ancient Vases . . . in the Possession of Sir William Hamilton* (first volume, 1791); James Tassie's engravings after classical cameos in R. E. Raspe, *Catalogue raisonné d'une collection générale de pierres gravées*, 1791. While the style of these publications announces itself in a work such as L. Begerus' *Thesaurus Brandenburgicus, sive gemmarum et numismatum . . . series* (Berlin, 1696), the engravings in the standard works on classi-

cal cameos published in the first half of the eighteenth century (e.g., Philippe de Stosch, *Pierres antiques gravées*, Amsterdam, 1724; Niccolò Galeotti, *Museum Odescalchum sive Thesaurus antiquarum gemmarum*, Rome, 1751; P. J. Mariette, *Traité de pierres gravées*, Paris, 1750) show very elaborate modeling.
[13] P.-F. d'Hancarville, *Antiquités étrusques, grecques et romaines, tirées du cabinet de M. Hamilton . . .* , Naples, 1766–1767.
[14] See the excellent article by A. Mongan, "Ingres and the Antique," *Journal of the Warburg and Courtauld Institutes*, x, 1947, pp. 1 ff.
[15] *Summa theologiae*, i, qu. 35, art. 1, c.
[16] See J. G. van Gelder, *Dilettanti en Kunstwetenschap*, Wormerveer, 1936, p. 20.

late eighteenth century not only established a professional tradition that lasted from Kilian, Tassie, and Tischbein through Clarac and Quatremère de Quincy down to Carl Robert and Salomon Reinach, but also inspired creative

42. John Flaxman: *Pandora Brought to Earth by Mercury*

artists from Philipp Otto Runge, Asmus Carstens, and Peter Cornelius through Ingres down to Matisse and Picasso.[17]

One of the earliest, and certainly the most influential, of these dedicated linearists was John Flaxman, "der Abgott aller Dilettanten," as Goethe calls him as early as 1799; [18] his illustrations of Homer (1793) and Aeschylus (1794) may be said to have crystallized the popular conception of a purely

[17] See, in addition to Mongan, *op. cit.*, J. Momméja, "La Jeunesse d'Ingres," *Gazette des Beaux-Arts*, ser. 3, xx, 1898, pp. 188 ff.; W. Friedlaender, *David to Delacroix*, Cambridge, Mass., 1952 (first published in German in 1930), p. 70.

[18] "Ueber die Flaxmanischen Werke," *Propyläen, zweiten Bandes erstes Stück*, 1799 (*Goethes Kunstschriften*, ii, pp. 193 ff.).

"Grecian" antiquity. Yet Flaxman's style is anything but Classicism pure and simple. Like every other master praised or condemned as a Classicist, he synthesized the antique with other, postclassical elements; but he applied a different principle of selection. Where Poussin had fused a substantial and, if one may say so, "lavish" antique (the antique of Praxitelian statuary, Roman sarcophagi, and Greco-Roman painting) with equally substantial and "lavish" manifestations of modern art (Raphael, the Venetians, even Bernard Salomon or Bernini), Flaxman chose, from both epochs, the attenuated and the abstemious. Blending the impression of "Etruscan" vase painting and ancient cameos with that of the Italian primitives (Goethe shrewdly commented upon his "gift of immersing himself in the innocent mood of the earlier Italian schools"), he was both a pupil of the antiquarians and a teacher of the Pre-Raphaelites. His line engravings, infused with a subjective sentiment that makes it hard to spot actual "borrowings," occasionally verge on the smooth prettiness of Wedgwood plaques (he worked, in fact, for Wedgwood for some time); but in happier moments they manage to evoke some of the spirit that illumines Keats's *Endymion*—or, for that matter, Goethe's *Pandora*, which, incidentally, was embellished by a modest German artist, Vincenz Raimund Grüner (1771–1832), with four unmistakably Flaxmanian illustrations (*fig. 43*).[19] And it is to Flaxman's genius that we owe the earliest and most complete interpretation of the Pandora myth as a detailed, cyclical narrative.[20]

[19] See Thieme-Becker, *op. cit.*, xv, p. 13; H. G. Gräf, *Goethe und seine Dichtungen*, ii, 4, Frankfurt, 1908, p. 22. In both places the information about Grüner's Pandora illustrations contains a slight error. According to Thieme-Becker, Grüner's engravings are found in the first edition of Goethe's *Pandora* (1808), whereas they do occur in the second: *Pandora von Goethe; Ein Taschenbuch für das Jahr 1810*, Vienna and Trieste (Geistingersche Buchhandlung). According to Gräf, the second engraving, reproduced in our *fig. 43*, shows "Pandora Bending over the Dreaming Epimetheus," whereas the female figure is in fact his and her daughter Elpore, "den Morgenstern auf dem Haupte, in luftigem Gewande" (Goethe, *Pandora*, 320–348; cf. below, p. 128). In a lecture delivered on November 21, 1953 (*Kunstgeschichtliche Gesellschaft zu Berlin, Sitzungsberichte*, Sept. 1953—May 1954, p. 5 f.), E. Redslob suggests an influence of Flaxman on Goethe himself, "vor allem auf Bildvorstellungen, aus denen das Fragment Pandora entstand." This, however, is at variance with Goethe's rather unenthusiastic attitude toward Flaxman and, even more so, with the fact that the latter's Hesiod illustrations were not published until 1817.

[20] For the much less comprehensive cycle by Henry Howard, see below, pp. 102 ff.

43. VINCENZ RAIMUND GRÜNER: *Elpore Appearing to Epimetheus*

Flaxman's six drawings, engraved by William Blake, form a coherent series within his *Compositions from the Works, Days and Theogony of Hesiod* (scheduled for publication in 1816 and actually printed in the following year),[21] one scene from the *Theogony* being interpolated into five from the *Works and Days.* The text employed and partly quoted in the legends is the

[21] Some of the engravings show the imprint "Published . . . November, 1816."

second edition (1815) of Charles Abraham Elton's translation, first published in 1812; [22] but in his legends Flaxman took some liberties with his source, not only for reasons of space but also in order to blunt the edge of Hesiod's animosity toward his "beautiful mischief."

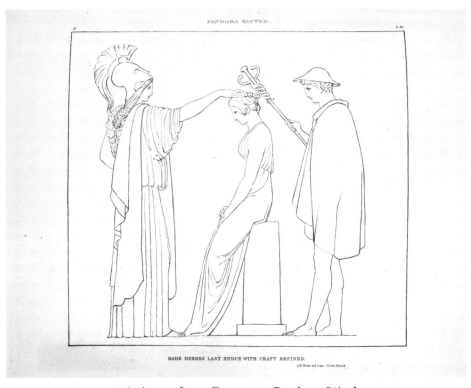

44. AFTER JOHN FLAXMAN: Pandora Gifted

In the first of his designs (*Pandora Gifted: fig. 44*) the text is edited in such a manner that those who do not remember the context are led to interpret the scene as something rather different from what the poet intended it to be. The virginal Pandora, fresh from the workshop of Hephaestus, is being endowed with psychological as well as physical life. Perhaps familiar with a

[22] C. A. Elton, *The Remains of Hesiod Translated from the Greek into English Verses*, London, 1812; second edition (from which we quote), London, 1815. That Flaxman used the second edition is evident from such deviations as that in the legend of the fourth scene (our *fig. 47*). This reads: "He bade Heaven's messenger convey thro' air / To Epemetheus' [*sic*] hands," whereas the first edition has: "The Sire commands the winged herald bear / The finished nymph . . ."

vase resembling the famous Blade Kylix in the British Museum (*frontis-piece*),[23] Flaxman reduced the number of the gods entrusted with this task to two: Pallas Athene, who places a wreath upon Pandora's hair, and Hermes, who with his caduceus touches her head from behind. Judging from the legend

PANDORA ATTIRED.

ADORED PERSUASION AND THE GRACES YOUNG
HER SLENDER LIMBS WITH GOLDEN JEWELS HUNG.

45. After John Flaxman: *Pandora Attired*

(*Works and Days*, 67), the spectator cannot but assume that this touch of the magic wand spells good rather than evil: "Bade Hermes last endue with craft refined." The complete sentence, however, reads:

> *Bade Hermes last implant the gift refined*
> *Of thievish manner and a shameless mind;*

[23] Roscher, *op. cit.*, III, cols. 1525–1526; a better illustration in A. S. Murray and A. H. Smith, *White Athenian Vases in the British Museum*, London, 1896, Plate 19. The Blade Kylix itself, apart from the fact that it shows Pallas Athene juxtaposed with Hephaestus rather than Hermes, cannot have been known to Flaxman if it is true that it was not found until *c.* 1828.

and even this is a fairly genteel paraphrase of Hesiod's ἐν δὲ θέμεν κύνεόν τε νόον καὶ ἐπίκλοπον ἦθος.

The following design, *Pandora Attired,* shows Pandora adorned by the three Graces while the Hours, carrying flowers and looking like Fra Angelico

46. AFTER JOHN FLAXMAN: *Pandora Shewn to the Gods*

angels rather than classical Horae, approach in flight and "adored Persuasion" stands quietly by (*fig. 45*); the legend repeats *Works and Days*, line 73, with only a slight verbal modification.[24]

The third composition, *Pandora Shewn to the Gods* (*fig. 46*), is based on the *Theogony*, so that Hephaestus—who in the *Works and Days* vanishes from the scene as soon as he has turned over his masterpiece to the other

[24] "Adored Persuasion and the Graces young / Her slender limbs with golden Jewels hung" instead of "With chains of gold her shapely person hung." The "beauteous-tressèd Hours," crowning Pandora's head with spring flowers, appear in the following line.

divinities for animation and adornment—is introduced as the proud artist "bringing out" the finished product and earning general admiration. But in the legend the second of the two lines describing this incident (*Theogony*,

47. AFTER JOHN FLAXMAN: *Pandora Brought to Earth*

588 ff.) is omitted; once more disapprobation has been turned into praise. On Flaxman's print, we read only:

> *On Men and Gods in that same moment seized*
> *The Ravishment of wonder when they saw.*

Without consulting the text no one would suspect that in the following line the object of this "ravishment of wonder" is defined as "the deep deceit, th' inextricable snare."

    Pandora Brought to Earth (*fig. 47*) may, at first glance, be thought to have been inspired by the translator's amplification of the Greek original:

where Hesiod (*Works and Days*, 83 ff.) says only that Zeus sent Hermes to Epimetheus, taking Pandora with him as a gift, Elton translates:

> *He bade Heaven's messenger convey* thro' air
> *To Epimetheus' hands . . .*

In this case, however, Flaxman seems to have drawn inspiration from a pictorial tradition represented by Jacob de Wit's *Apotheosis of Psyche* (*fig. 7*) rather than from the text: he had interpreted the incident as a magnificent flight through space as early as 1805, seven years before even the first edition of Elton's translation, when he exhibited at the Royal Academy a silver relief entitled *Mercury Descending with Pandora*, supposedly destined for a vase commemorating the dead of Trafalgar and known to us through several replicas in plaster (*fig. 42*). Apart from such minor changes as the addition of little wings to the feet and cap of Mercury and the elaboration of Pandora's wreath or fillet into a crenelated diadem, the engraving of 1816 so closely follows this relief that it has been mistaken for the latter's prototype.[25] It should be noted, furthermore, that the legend of Flaxman's print again omits the unflattering implications of the passage quoted; the second line, cut in half without any gain from a typographical point of view, reads *in toto:* "To Epimetheus' hands th' inextricable snare."

Next comes *Pandora Brought to Epimetheus* according to *Works and Days*, 87 ff. (*fig. 48*), and it is in this scene—the scene so naïvely interpreted as a middle-class idyl in Pieter Serwouters' engraving—that the "fatal vessel" makes its appearance. In a work by Flaxman this vessel might be expected either to be rendered with at least the same degree of archaeological con-

[25] See E. B. Chancellor, *The Lives of the British Sculptors*, London, 1911, p. 253. The correct dates are found in W. C. Constable, *John Flaxman*, London, 1927, pp. 68, 90; see also A. T. Bolton, *Description of . . . the Residence of Sir John Soane* (eleventh edition of the Official Handbook of Sir John Soane's Museum), Oxford, 1930, p. 76, fig. 44. To Mr. John Summerson, Curator of Sir John Soane's Museum, we are very grateful for the photograph reproduced in *fig. 42*, as well as for information to the effect that the Soane's Museum owns, in addition to the small plaque here reproduced (S.C. 46), a nearly identical one of larger size (S.C. 948); and that two others are at the University College, London (T. Ely, *Catalogue of Works of Art in the Flaxman Gallery, University College, London*, London, 1900, Nos. 3 and 40, pp. 8 and 20).

scientiousness as Bonasone's stamnos (*fig. 39*) or to conform to that ideal of Grecian nobility which Goethe expressed by the phrase "des irdenen Gefässes hohe Wohlgestalt." [26] Such, however, is not the case. Flaxman's pithos neither

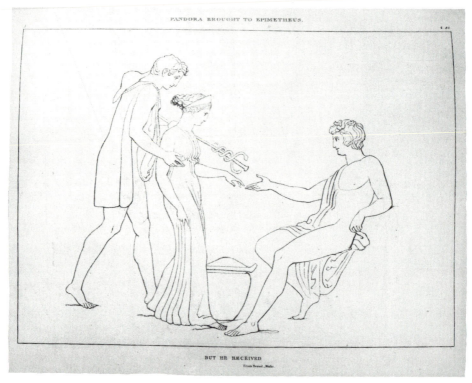

48. AFTER JOHN FLAXMAN: *Pandora Brought to Epimetheus*

corresponds to any of the orthodox types of classical pottery, nor does it deserve such laudatory epithets as "tall" and "shapely." It is, in fact, a rather dumpy vessel that in archaeological terms can be described, at best, as a cross between a Greek *lebes* and a prehistoric Italian ash urn.[27] It manages, however, to look convincing as an implement both "Hellenic" and "primitive" (since Flaxman needed a covered vessel evocative of a primordial stage of civilization, the combination of *lebes* and ash urn may even have been inten-

[26] Goethe, *Pandora*, 93; an earlier variant is "Das ird'ne, hohe, wohlgestaltete Gefäss."
[27] For the latter, see, e.g., O. Montelius, *La Civilisation primitive en Italie depuis l'introduction des métaux*, I, Stockholm, 1895, Plate 58, No. 11, or Plate 59, No. 19.

tional). More important, it occupies, for the first time, its legitimate place in the narrative, and both these things are the more remarkable as Flaxman's source, the second edition of Elton's translation, still portrays Pandora as the conveyor of the pithos and even speaks of it, in alternation, as a "vessel,"

49. AFTER JOHN FLAXMAN: *Pandora Opening the Vase*

a "coffer," and a "casket" ("The woman's hands an ample cascet bear").[28] In Flaxman's composition, as in all classical literature, its presence is taken for granted. No longer thought of as being in Pandora's personal custody, it simply sits on the ground between the admiring, welcoming groom and the lovely, reluctant bride—a silent menace unperceived by either.

In the sixth and last of Flaxman's designs, *Pandora Opening the Vase* (*fig. 49*), the menace has become a reality. The pithos—in its shape and

---

[28] *Works and Days*, lines 94, 97, 98. Only where the Greek text has δόμοισιν (line 96) does the second edition of Elton's translation have "vase." In the first edition, the word πίθος (only alluded to by a "within" in the rendering of line 97) is twice translated as "cascet" (lines 94 and 93), while the ἀρρήκτοισι δόμοισιν is translated as "th' unbroken cell."

construction oddly inconsistent with its appearance in the preceding scene [29] —is shifted slightly to the right. Kneeling before it and looking up with an expression of bland incomprehension rather than either curiosity or fear, Pandora has lifted the large lid (indeed a μέγα πῶμα; in fact, too wide to fit the vessel's mouth) and "scatters ills in air." Epimetheus, in a violent *contrapposto* movement skillfully contrived from two classical motifs never combined in one classical figure, the "pathos pose" of the dying Orpheus and the lunge of the fighter, turns away in a panic-stricken effort at escaping from the Diseases and the other Evils—the former represented as tiny skeletons like Roman larvae, the latter well formed but viciously aggressive—which rush forth from the vase. And Hope, a small, frail figure proffering a flower, is visible inside as though her "unbroken home" were made of glass.

Barry and Flaxman, then, endeavored to restore to the Hesiodian pithos the rights so long usurped by the Erasmian pyxis, and their reformatory zeal was shared by a third English artist, Henry Howard, who in 1834 decorated the ceiling of the dining room in the house of Sir John Soane (now Sir John Soane's Museum) in London with what seems to be the only surviving cyclical rendering of the Pandora myth in painting (*fig. 50*).[30] He told her story in three pictures separated by two oblong panels that show, respectively, the Times of Day, viz., Morning, Midday, and Evening (their attributes suggesting, at the same time, Spring, Summer, and Autumn), and Night (analogously suggestive of Winter) surrounded by the Pleiades. In the central picture (*fig. 51*), manifestly dependent on Barry's giant canvas at Manchester, we see Pandora endowed with the gifts of the gods, the Fates attending upon Jupiter, who holds the fatal vessel on his knees, Vulcan proudly standing by, and Mercury putting on his winged sandals for the flight to earth. This flight

---

[29] In the first Epimetheus scene (*fig. 48*) the body of the vessel is high-shouldered like that of a *lebes,* and the cover is shaped like an inverted bowl, its rim projecting beyond the mouth of the vessel. In the second scene (*fig. 49*) the vessel has no shoulder but opens up like a skyphos; the cover is flat; and the same projection that in the first illustration represents the rim of the cover here belongs to the silhouette of the vessel itself.

[30] Howard's panels, still *in situ* but thus far unpublished, are described in Bolton, *op. cit.,* p. 33. This description was brought to our attention by Mr. John Summerson, to whom we are also indebted for kindly providing us with photographs. For a lost cycle executed under the supervision of Velázquez, see "Addenda to the Second Edition," pp. 161 ff.

50. Henry Howard: Ceiling decoration

52. HENRY HOWARD: *Pandora Brought to Epimetheus by Mercury*

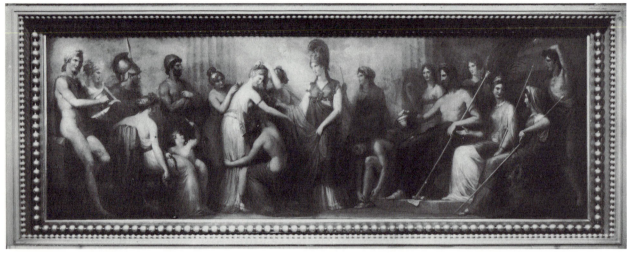

51. HENRY HOWARD: *Pandora Endowed with the Gifts of the Gods*

53. HENRY HOWARD: *Epimetheus Opening Pandora's Vase*

is represented in the lunette-shaped picture on the west side (*fig. 52*), as evidently influenced by Flaxman as the central picture is by Barry—except for the fact that Pandora brings the vessel with her instead of encountering it upon her arrival, and that the composition includes a very un-Flaxmanian, exuberantly welcoming Epimetheus. The lunette on the opposite side (*fig. 53*), finally, shows Epimetheus opening the vase while Pandora shrinks from the escaping evils in helpless terror.

For all his classicizing intentions, Howard thus reverted to the "Philo-demus-Erasmus variant" according to which Pandora in person transports the vase from Mount Olympus to earth but leaves its opening to her husband. And this is all the more remarkable as the vase itself, a kind of volute krater with fluted cover in the central panel, is represented as an altogether different vessel, namely, a fairly orthodox stamnos, in both of the lunettes. Would it be too hazardous to assume that Howard had chanced upon the Bonasone print, which seems to be the only rendering to show a stamnos opened by a gentleman?

Soon, however, idiom triumphed over archaeology.[31] And it was especially in the English-speaking countries that art put the finishing touch to the Erasmian heresy: "Pandora's box" came to be imagined and represented in a form entirely exceptional before (*fig. 62*) but now most naturally coming to mind when the familiar phrase is heard, as a receptacle varying in size from that of a jewel box to that of a sailor's sea chest (and tending to be elaborated into a precious, often richly ornamented, *objet d'art*) but rectangular rather than rounded in shape.[32]

[31] The "box" still haunts even some scholarly discussions (cf. n. 2, p. 3), not to mention such popular paraphrases as that in E. Hamilton, *Mythology* (Mentor Books edition, New York, 1953), p. 70, with a preposterous illustration by Steele Savage.

[32] On the European continent, the representation of Pandora's box as a round object varying in shape and size between a vase or goblet and a pillbox or lady's compact subsisted throughout the nineteenth century and even beyond; suffice it to mention, apart from a statue in three-quarter length by the con-temporary Flemish sculptor, Jan Antennis (privately owned), a painting by the German painter Nathanael Sichel (died 1907) that has had the undeserved honor of being included in the "revised edition" of T. Bulfinch's justly popular *The Age of Fable or Beauties of Mythology* (Philadelphia, 1898, p. 22). To make confusion worse confounded, Bulfinch's originally unimpeachable account of the myth has here been encumbered with a quotation from Longfellow's *Masque of Pandora* (written 1875, performed at Boston in 1881), which reads: "Yon mysterious [should read 'oaken']

54. JEAN-PIERRE CORTOT:
Pandora

The earliest examples of this final innovation are, as far as we could ascertain, two works nearly contemporary in date but very different in character: a coolly academic marble statue by Jean-Pierre Cortot (the author of the formerly popular *Messenger of Marathon*); and a large painting by William Etty that, though equally academic, is anything but cool. Cortot's statue, shown at the Paris Salon of 1819 and now preserved in the Musée des Beaux-Arts at Lyons (*fig. 54*),[33] opens a series of nineteenth-century works in which Pandora's name and attribute are little more than an excuse for representing an attractive nude or deminude, demure in this particular instance, not so demure in others. Etty's painting, exhibited at the Royal Academy in 1824 and recently acquired by Temple Newsam House at Leeds (*fig. 55*),[34] is characteristic of an artist whom many of his contemporaries and most of his

chest / Carven with figures and embossed with gold." We have not tried to trace a number of French statues shown at the Paris Salon from 1842 to 1864 and listed in Larousse, *loc. cit.* (by Auguste Famin, James Pradier, Antoine Desboeufs, François-Clément Moreau, Jean Bulio, Pierre Loison, Auguste Moreau, Pierre-Alfred Robinet, and Jean Valette); it is not difficult to imagine how they look. As an American parallel there may be mentioned a marble statue by Chauncey B. Ives (1812–1894, mostly active in Italy from 1844) that adorns the Blue Parlor in the Harral House at Bridgeport, Connecticut (illustrated in E. Donnell, "A. J. Davis and the Gothic Revival," *Metropolitan Museum Studies*, V, 2, 1936, pp. 183 ff., fig. 35). We wish to thank Professor J. F. Kienitz for having called our attention to this article, and to Mr. Wayne Andrews for having informed us of the identity of the artist (cf. Thieme-Becker, *op. cit.*, XIX, p. 369, and *Dictionary of American Biography*, IX, p. 518, both with incorrect birth dates). As we learn from Mr. Thomas J. McCormick, Jr., a replica of the Bridgeport *Pandora* is in the Virginia Museum of Art at Richmond.

[33] See Larousse, *loc. cit.*; Thieme-Becker, *op. cit.*, VII, p. 498, with the information that Cortot's statue is based upon a drawing by François-Louis Dejuinne, a pupil of Girodet's.
[34] See *Leeds Art Calendar*, VIII, No. 26, Summer, 1954, pp. 6 f. Our thanks are due to Mr. E. I. Musgrave, Director of Temple Newsam House, Leeds, for permission to reproduce the painting.

55. Wᴵʟʟᴵᴀᴍ Eᴛᴛʏ: *Pandora Crowned by the Horae*

juniors despised as a "flesh painter." Combining the basic features of the van Diepenbeeck-Bloemaert composition with reminiscences of Venetian Renaissance painting, Etty shows Pandora crowned by the Horae [35] while Vulcan (seen from the rear after the fashion of van Diepenbeeck's Neptune) casts an admiring glance upon his work. The lower left-hand corner is occupied by a "Venus Embracing Cupid," and from the upper right Mercury flies in with the new small, square model of the fateful box.

The heroine's inviting physique, ambiguous pose, and yearning expression make this strange painting—which so strongly appealed to Sir Thomas Lawrence that he forthwith bought it from the Academy Exhibition and kept it in his home up to his death—the harbinger of a further development, no less characteristically English than Pandora's sanctification at the hands of

[35] We prefer this somewhat indefinite term to "Seasons," as the *Leeds Art Calendar* has it.

56 and *57*. Dante Gabriel Rossetti: *Pandora*

Flaxman and, at the same time, no less characteristically Victorian than the demonization of the *Mona Lisa* at the hands of Walter Pater: in a composition by Dante Gabriel Rossetti transmitted, with minor variations, through three or four different drawings and two oil paintings (*figs. 56* and *57*),[36] she

[36] Mr. D. Loshak (*College Art Journal*, XVI, 1959, pp. 259 ff.) has corrected several errors in our account of Rossetti's Pandora compositions; but even now the problem of their whereabouts remains unsolved in most cases. This applies particularly to the famous picture completed for Rossetti's faithful patron, William Graham, in 1871 and later owned by Mr. Charles Butler (H. C. Marillier, *Dante Gabriel Rossetti*, 2nd ed., London, 1901, No. 310, plate facing p. 118, our *fig. 56*): only from the descriptions do we learn that the narrower side of the box is inscribed *Nescitur ignescitur* (which is even worse than *Ultima manet Spes*) and that the frame displays the first two lines of Rossetti's sonnet. The crayon drawing reproduced in our *fig. 57* was not, as stated, produced in 1869 but is "either a variant or, more probably, early unfinished state" of a drawing now preserved in the Fogg Museum at Cambridge (Marillier, *ed. cit.*, No. 375) and made in preparation of a later pic-

becomes the *femme fatale*. Voluptuously sentimental and sentimentally volup-
tous, embellished by that superabundance of hair which is the very signa-
ture of the Pre-Raphaelite conception of beauty, she transfixes the beholder
with a deep look from shadowed eyes while spasmodically holding down the
lid of a precious little box from which the evil spirits escape in a smoky cloud.
The box is made of gold, either plain or bejeweled; and in one version it
even exhibits the image of Hope, reduced to an angelic head, ecstatically
raised, and identified by the semiliterate inscription VLTIMA MANET SPES.[37]

In 1955, it is not easy to take such pictures entirely seriously; but the
temper of the times may change again, and our children or grandchildren
may be able to re-experience some of the feelings with which Rossetti's *Pandora* inspired his friend Swinburne, not to mention himself. "The whole
design," writes Swinburne, "is among Rossetti's mightiest in godlike terror
and imperial trouble of beauty, shadowed by the smoke and fiery vapour of
winged and fleshless passions crowding from the cascet in spires of flame-lit
and curling cloud round her fatal face and mourning veil of hair." [38] Rossetti himself devoted to his composition the following sonnet:

> *What of the end, Pandora? Was it thine,*
> *The deed that set these fiery pinions free?*
> *Ah! wherefore did the Olympian consistory*
> *In its own likeness make thee half divine?*
> *Was it that Juno's brow might stand a sign*
> *Forever? and the mien of Pallas be*
> *A deadly thing? and that all men might see*
> *In Venus' eyes the gaze of Proserpine?*

---

ture, dated 1879, which Evelyn Waugh (*Rossetti; His Life and Works*, London, 1928, p.
190) describes as exhibiting a "disagreeable
contrast between the massive modelling of the
bare shoulder and the exaggerated spirituality
of the face"; and the drawing formerly owned
by Mr. T. Eustace Smith is, according to Mr.
Loshak, a free repetition of this later drawing.
The work illustrated in Arthur Symons, *Dante
Gabriel Rossetti* (Kunst der Gegenwart, II, 3,
Berlin, 1909), p. 44, finally, is identical with

a crayon drawing (Marillier, *ed. cit.*, No. 281)
made, in 1869, in preparation of the Graham-
Butler picture. A signed water-color version of
this earlier drawing exists in the Art Museum
at Princeton, N. J.; see "Addenda to the Second Edition," p. 166, and *fig. 67.*
[37] For the correct wording, see above, p. 39.
[38] Swinburne's eulogy, from *Essays and
Studies*, is here quoted after E. Wood, *Dante
Rossetti and the Pre-Raphaelite Movement*,
London, 1894, p. 242.

What of the end? these beat their wings at will,
The ill-born things, the good things turned to ill—
Powers of the impassioned hours prohibited.
Aye, hug the cascet now! Whither they go
Thou may'st not dare to think: nor canst thou know
If Hope still pent there be alive or dead.[39]

Nathaniel Hawthorne, representing the opposite aspect of Anglo-Saxon Victorianism, rewrote the Hesiodian myth in a spirit of childlike innocence

58. AFTER HAMMATT BILLINGS:
Pandora Opening the Box

that strikes the modern reader as no less brittle than Rossetti's pseudo-Baudelairean preoccupation with sin. Hawthorne's paraphrase, leaving an ineffaceable impression on the youthful minds of countless Anglo-Saxon

[39] Dante Gabriel Rossetti, *Poems*, Boston, Stephens, *Dante Gabriel Rossetti*, London, 1870, p. 272 (also reprinted, e.g., in F. G. 1894).

readers, is a fairy tale for children, illustrated by one of Hammatt Billings' rather appealing, if overly pretty, wood engravings (*fig. 58*). Pandora was a little girl sent as a "playfellow and helpmate" to Epimetheus, who "was a very good-tempered child." "The first thing she saw was a great box. And almost the first question which she put to him . . . was this: 'Epimetheus, what have you in that box?' " The question preys on both their minds: "The box, the box, and nothing but the box. . . ." "She had called it ugly about a hundred times, but . . . it was positively a very handsome article of furniture, made of a beautiful kind of wood, with dark and rich veins spreading over its surface, which was so highly polished that little Pandora could see her face in it." Edges and corners were carved with wonderful skill, the carvings showing "figures of graceful men and women, and the prettiest children ever seen reclining or sporting amid a profusion of foliage." The temptation of this marvelous box (fastened, "not by a lock but by a very intricate knot of gold cord") proves, of course, irresistible, and Pandora opens it while Epimetheus does nothing to prevent her. The Troubles, in the shape of sharp-stinged insects, escape, and the children close the lid in terror. But little Hope, described as a kind of fairy, wants to be let out—a new and rather shrewd correction of Hesiod's illogical conclusion—and this is done by both children in conjunction. So "the Troubles and Hope are both loose in the world." [40]

*

IN THE twentieth century two prominent postimpressionist artists have tried to recapture the pessimistic implications of the Hesiodian tale and to restate them with reference to the more lurid aspects of our own civilization: Paul Klee and Max Beckmann. Both, characteristically, obliterated the heroine and employed Pandora's box as a kind of independent hieroglyph. Paul Klee,

[40] Nathaniel Hawthorne, *Wonder-Book for Girls and Boys*, Boston, 1852, pp. 98 ff. For a silly imitation of Hawthorne's tale, see *Pandora, Retold by Mary Patric* (illustrated by Erika Weihs), Kenosha, Wisconsin, n. d.

59. Paul Klee: *"Die Büchse der Pandora als Stilleben"*

60. Max Beckmann: *Pandora's Box*

ironically inscribing his little drawing (dated 1920) *Die Büchse der Pandora als Stilleben* and, perhaps unbeknownst to himself, reviving two rather time-worn traditions at the same time,[41] represented the ominous receptacle as a kind of goblet rather than a box and converted it into a psychoanalytical symbol: it is rendered as a kantharos-shaped vase containing some flowers but emitting evil vapors from an opening clearly suggestive of the female genitals (*fig. 59*).[42] Max Beckmann's gouache, begun in 1936 but thoroughly repainted in 1947, first anticipated and then recorded the horrors of the atomic bomb: his "Pandora's box" is a small, square object charged with an incalculable amount of energy and exploding into a chaos of shattered form and color (*fig. 60*).[43]

With these contemporary productions the representational evolution has run full cycle. Beginning with the emblem books, where, we remember, Pandora's cask, and only her cask, appears as an attribute of Hope, it ends with two renderings in which Pandora's box, and only her box, appears as a symbol of misery and destruction.

[41] For the idea of representing Pandora's box as a little vase or goblet, see above, pp. 19 ff.; for its interpretation as a sex symbol, see the texts reprinted in n. 21, p. 77, and n. 1, p. 79.

[42] *Paul Klee, Exhibition Catalogue, Buchholz Gallery, New York, May 2–27, 1950,* No. 2 (not illustrated). The late Mr. Curt Valentin obliged us by providing us with a photograph.

[43] So far as we know, Max Beckmann's picture has not been published or referred to in print. We owe the information and the photograph to its present owner, who wishes to remain anonymous.

A more explicit reference to nuclear weapons is found in a cartoon by L. J. Jordaan (see Thieme-Becker, *op. cit.*, xix, p. 150) published in *Vrij Nederland, Onafhankelijk Weekblad*, xv, August 13, 1955, and kindly brought to our attention, like so many other interesting items, by Professor J. G. van Gelder. It shows "The World" seated on a bench, with a huge, square box, inscribed ATOOM, on its lap. From the box there escape three bombs equipped with bat's wings and appropriately labeled (A-BOM, H-BOM, COBALT BOM), as well as a dove bearing an olive branch and a scroll inscribed "Vreedzam Gebruik Atoom-Energie" ("Peaceful Use of Atomic Energy"). The caption reads: "De doos van Pandora: 'Kommt ein Vogel geflogen.'"

EPILOGUE

Pandora on the Stage

Pandora on the Stage:

Calderón, Voltaire, Goethe, and

Late-Antique Allegory

N o t long before Isaac de Benserade included the myth of Pandora in his *Ovide en rondeaux* (because this fable, though absent from the *Metamorphoses,* was "trop celebre pour n'y estre pas inséree"),[1] she had made her appearance on the theatrical stage. And here—provided that the intention of the playwrights transcended that of purveying such lighthearted, witty entertainment as was offered in the Théâtres de la Foire at Paris [2]—she tended to be invested with a variety of allegorical meanings. Seen in motivated interaction with other personages and personifications rather than operating as an

[1] See n. 1, p. 79.

[2] For the Théâtres de la Foire, swept into prominence after the expulsion of the Italian Comedians in 1697 and, even after the latter's readmission in 1716, continuing to operate in lively competition with the Comédie Française and the Opéra Française, see D. Panofsky, "Gilles or Pierrot? Iconographic Notes on Watteau," *Gazette des Beaux-Arts*, ser. 6, xxxix, 1952, pp. 319 ff., with further references. Between 1721 and 1729 the Forains staged three Pandora plays, all entitled *La Boîte de Pandore* (Claude and François Parfaict, *Dictionnaire des Théâtres de Paris*, 1756, IV, p. 66): one by de Santfois, performed in 1721, one by Philippe Poisson, performed in 1729, and one by Le Sage and d'Orneval (Le Sage and d'Orneval, *Le Théâtre de la Foire*, IV, Paris, 1724, pp. 377 ff.). Suffice it to summarize the last-named, a "comédie en un acte et en prose," performed in 1724. Questioned by Pierrot, Pandora informs him that she is in reality a marble statue fashioned by Vulcan but

subsequently animated and provided with her little box by Jupiter. When Pierrot attempts to peek into the box, she bravely resists and finds herself supported by Mercury, who— "sous la forme de Harlequin"—descends from Mount Olympus for the special purpose of keeping the box inviolate until the proper moment. This moment comes when Pierrot is about to marry a girl named Olivette. Everybody, including mothers, aunts, cousins, and even the former sweethearts of Pierrot and Olivette, is cheerful, generous, and forgiving— until Pandora presents her box to Olivette as a wedding gift. When it is opened, the atmosphere is poisoned by ill will, cupidity, and jealousy, with the result that the wrong people get married. And after a witty dig at the restrictions imposed upon the Forains in favor of their more respectable rivals ("Il nous est défendu de dancer; nous vous avions préparé un Divertissement complet mais l'Envie qui est sortie de la Boête de Pandore pour aller à l'Opéra nous oblige à vous donner des

instrument of fate, she ceased to be an *exemplum* and became a *similitudo:* instead of typifying a concrete, affective experience—the experience of feminine perfection, feminine destructiveness, or a combination of both—she "manifested," as Thomas Aquinas would say, an abstract, philosophical concept.

This new development is ushered in, apparently without much precedent, by Calderón's *La Estatua de Prometeo,* one of those "fiestas," strangely combining the features of the Mannerist *intermedio* with those of the Baroque opera and the bucolic comedy, which were performed at the Buen Retiro for Philip IV.[3] In accordance with the prevailing, non-Hesiodian tradition, Calderón's Pandora is a beautiful statue fashioned by Prometheus; but in contrast to all previous versions, this statue is not the corporeal substratum of a "first woman" but the cult image of a goddess. Illumined by the spirit of sculpture as well as philosophy, Prometheus has conceived it as a likeness of "Minerva," a deity whom Calderón not only separates from, but diametrically opposes to, "Pallas." Far from being one and the same, "Minerva" and "Pallas" (who explains the situation in a speech of eighty lines) are twin sisters, both beautiful and mighty but representing contradictory, if complementary, principles: "Minerva," traditionally the "patron saint" of Prometheus, stands for the arts and sciences, which, according to "Pallas," breed sacrilegious pride; "Pallas" stands for military pursuits, which, according to her, serve to develop true courage and religious humility.

Quite naturally, "Pallas" wants the image of her rival destroyed; but, equally naturally, "Minerva" wants it to be animated so as to take an active part in the affairs of the world. Thus, she helps Prometheus to appropriate a

---

Comédies toutes nues"), the play ends with a terzetto sung by the newlyweds and Mercury-Harlequin:

> *Mère qui vit trop librement*
> *Devant sa Fille neuve encore,*
> *Ouvre au Tendron imprudemment*
> *La Boête de Pandore.*
> *Deux Amans vivent dans l'erreur:*
> *Tout est charmant quand on s'adore;*
> *Mais l'hymen ouvre par malheur*
> *La Boête de Pandore.*
> *Cachez si bien vos soins jaloux,*

> *Que votre Femme les ignore;*
> *N'ouvrez point, indiscrets Epoux,*
> *La Boête de Pandore.*
> [*aux spectateurs:*]
> *Souvent l'un gagne et l'autre perd:*
> *Si d'un bené l'on nous honore,*
> *A profit nous aurons ouvert*
> *La Boête de Pandore.*

[3] *Las comedias de D. Pedro Calderón de la Barca,* J. J. Keil, ed., III, Leipzig, 1829, pp. 321 ff.; cf. E. Günthner, *Calderón und seine Werke,* Freiburg, 1888, I, pp. 296 ff.

ray from Apollo's sun, which transforms the statue into a living thing—a living thing that wins the love of Prometheus himself as well as of his brother, Epimetheus, and is acclaimed by all with the name "Pandora," explained by the jealous and etymologically untutored "Pallas" as signifying "Providencia del Tiempo." Calderón's Pandora, then, is a visible and tangible manifestation of the goddess "Minerva" (she is, in fact, herself referred to as "Minerva" as soon as she has ceased to be a lifeless statue), and this determines all further events, especially the very unorthodox denouement. Having failed in enlisting the help of Epimetheus, "Pallas" causes "Discordia," disguised as a peasant woman, to present Pandora with a deceptively handsome vessel (*dorada urna*), which, when opened by the unsuspecting recipient, emits dark fumes that spread all over the scene. General confusion and hostility ensue. Prometheus flees from his own creature, although she dearly loves him, while Epimetheus pursues her, although she does not care for him. A terrible battle begins between the two brothers and their adherents, and all sing in dispair: "Woe to him who saw good change to bad, and bad to worse."

But in the end the real "Minerva" prevails upon Apollo to forgive Prometheus' theft and to dispel the fumes of discord by the divine light of his sun. The brothers are reconciled; Prometheus—never before cast in the role of a loving husband [4]—marries Pandora; and all unite in a final song in which the earlier lament is turned into a paean of triumph: "Happy he who saw bad change to good, and good to better." Hope, of course, does not appear in Calderón's play at all, because the union between Prometheus and Pandora, the creative human mind and the ennobling, god-enlivened embodiment of art and science, has become a blissful reality.

*

At first glance, little or no connection seems to exist between this lofty-minded glorification of Pandora and the treatment she received in Voltaire's

---

[4] Unless one wishes to resurrect the obscure and isolated references to Deucalion as a son of Prometheus and Pandora (cf. n. 8, p. 7).

Pandore, an opera written in 1740, first printed in 1748, set to music by Jean-Benjamin de Laborde in 1765, translated into English by Thomas Francklin in 1772, but never performed on the stage.[5] Where Calderón extols Pandora as a reincarnation of Minerva, Voltaire presents her in the traditional role of the first woman whose action subjected mankind to all manner of evil. (He himself occasionally refers to his work as *Le Péché original* and calls it "un opéra philosophique qui devrait être joué devant Bayle et Diderot; il s'agit de l'origine du mal moral et du mal physique.")[6] Where Calderón celebrates her virtues in the name of spiritual enlightenment, Voltaire excuses, even exalts, her very frailty in the name of love. However, by means of this ingenious psychological twist, he manages to enlist the sympathies of the spectator and to ensure a happy ending (so that he thought his opera appropriate for presentation at royal weddings).[7] And he borrowed from Calderón, whom he admired with the same reservations as he did Shakespeare, and one of whose *comedias divinas*, the *Exaltación de la Cruz*, he translated into French,[8] not only this happy ending and such theatrical effects as the darkening of the stage after the box has been opened, but also two specific and important innovations: the exculpatory idea that the box is presented to Pandora by a malignant power in disguise (viz., by Nemesis disguised as Mercury, clearly a variation on Calderón's Discord disguised as a peasant woman), and the more fundamental notion that she and Prometheus are lovers.[9]

---

[5] See *Oeuvres complètes de Voltaire, Nouvelle édition conforme pour le texte à l'édition de Beuchot*, Paris, 1877–1885, III, pp. 574 ff. Francklin's translation, from which we quote a few lines in the text, appeared in *Dramatic Works of M. de Voltaire Translated by the Rev. Mr. Francklin*, XXII, London, 1772.

[6] *Oeuvres complètes de Voltaire*, XLVI, p. 98 (letter of November 4, 1765, to J.-B. de Laborde, asking him to compose the music for *Pandore*); for earlier, abortive plans in this direction, cf. *ibidem*, XXXVI, p. 37.

[7] Voltaire proposed performances of *Pandore* for the wedding of the Dauphin (later Louis XVI) in 1770, and for that of the Comte d'Artois (later Charles X) in 1773, both times without success; see *Oeuvres complètes*, III, p. 573.

[8] For Calderón's *Exaltación de la Cruz*, see Keil, *op. cit.*, III, pp. 632 ff., and Günthner, *op. cit.*, I, pp. 113 ff.; for Voltaire's translation, entitled *Héraclius*, see *Oeuvres complètes*, VII, pp. 491 ff. In Voltaire's opinion, both Shakespeare's and Calderón's plays represent "a mixture of ignorance and genius" (*ibidem*, VII, 435, 510, 535; XLII, p. 125).

[9] That Prometheus married Pandora is also taken for granted ("comme on sait") in Voltaire's more frivolous *Origine des Métiers* (*Oeuvres complètes*, X, p. 48 f.), which describes Prometheus as both *premier époux* and *le premier trompé* and derives the various occupations of mankind from Pandora's successive love affairs with Mars, Neptune, Apollo, Mercury, and Vulcan. Her own "métier," of course, "quoique peu rare, est encore le plus doux; / Et c'est celui que tout Paris honore."

When the scene opens, Pandora, as yet inanimate, "reclines on a platform" and Prometheus, like Pygmalion, yearns to embrace her as a living human being. But Jupiter (playing, in Voltaire's own words, "un assez indigne rôle, il ne lui manque que deux tonneaux")[10] refuses to the beautiful statue "the pow'r / To breathe, to think, to love, and to be happy." Prometheus, therefore, penetrates the heavens and lights his torch, not at the sun but at "love's sacred flame, more brilliant than the light / Of glitt'ring day and to Jove's boasted thunder / Superior." Touched with this flame, Pandora comes to life and reciprocates the love of Prometheus. But at the command of Jupiter she is abducted and transported to his palace, "brilliant with gold and light" but filling her with wonder rather than pleasure. Here she is promised—ex post facto, so to speak—all the gifts the gods have to bestow, including immortality; but she refuses all these and remains faithful to Prometheus, who, supported by the Titans, starts a war of liberation against the Olympians. Destiny separates the combatants and forces Jupiter to return Pandora to Prometheus. In order to take his revenge, Jupiter dispatches Nemesis, who, disguised as Mercury, presents Pandora with a golden box and tempts her to open it. And she, so brave and true in the face of direct bribery, succumbs in the belief that the box contains a secret charm that will eternalize her beauty and, therefore, the love of him who "est l'auteur de ma naissance, / Mon roi, mon amant, mon époux." In spite of Prometheus' injunction, she yields; but she yields only when Nemesis has played her trump card: "Au nom de la nature entière, / Au nom de votre époux, rendez-vous à ma voix." Thus, though not as blameless as Calderón's "Minerva," she cannot be judged harshly, because she sins for the sake of love and not out of curiosity or selfishness. She deserves to be saved; and she is saved by a *deus ex machina* who, most consistently, appears in the shape of Cupid rather than of Apollo. Descending from heaven and calling Hope to his assistance, Love conquers Jupiter as well as Fate. Prometheus and Pandora join in a duet:

---

[10] See Voltaire's letter to de Laborde referred to in n. 6, p. 120. The reference, apparently still current in eighteenth-century France, is, of course, to the two pithoi at the Gates of Jupiter (cf. above, pp. 48 ff.).

Le ciel en vain sur nous rassemble
Les maux, la crainte et l'horreur de mourir.
Nous souffrirons ensemble,
Et c'est ne point souffrir.

And the play ends with what may be called Pandora's Creed:

Des destins la chaîne redoutable
Nous entraine à d'éternels malheurs:
Mais l'espoir à jamais secourable
De ses mains viendra sécher nos pleurs.

Dans nos maux il sera des délices,
Nous aurons de charmants erreurs,
Nous serons au bord des précipices,
Mais l'amour les couvrira de fleurs.[11]

*

AT THE age of twenty-four, in 1773, Goethe wrote a Prometheus play that was destined to remain a *dramatisches Fragment:* only the first two acts were finished, while the third did not proceed beyond that magnificent challenge to the gods ("Bedecke deinen Himmel, Zeus, mit Wolkendunst") which, owing to its separate appearance in Goethe's *Poems* and, perhaps, to its being set to music by Schubert, is better known to modern readers than the rest.

Here Pandora is, quite traditionally, one of the many human beings created by Prometheus; she occupies, however, a privileged position from

---

[11] Voltaire's interest in Pandora lasted throughout his long life. In *Il faut prendre un parti* (1772) he wrote, much in the spirit of the final song of his opera: "Rien n'est plus spirituel et plus agréable, en effet, que le conte de Pandore et de sa boîte. . . . Cette boîte de Pandore, en contenant tous les maux qui en sont sortis, semble aussi renfermer tous les charmes des allusions les plus frappants à la fois et les plus délicats" (*Oeuvres complètes,* XXVIII, pp. 537 f.). And in the previous year, at the age of seventy-seven, he had made a "translation" of the pertinent Hesiod passage (*ibidem,* XVIII, p. 565) that reads into the Greek original not only the "Erasmian version" but also the Biblical account of the Fall of Man:

Il [Jupiter] envoie à Pandore un écrin précieux;
Sa forme et son éclat éblouissent les yeux;
Quels biens doit renfermer cette boîte si belle!
De la bonté des Dieux c'est un gage fidèle;
C'est là qu'est renfermé le sort du genre humain.
Nous serons tous des dieux. Elle l'ouvre; et soudain . . .

For "Pandore, mélodrame en vers, texte d'Aumale de Corsenville, musique de Franz Beck, représenté pour la première fois à Paris le 2 juillet 1789," see J. van der Veen, *Le Mélodrame musical de Rousseau au Romantisme,* The Hague, 1955, pp. 44–46.

the outset. When showing Minerva all the statues that he has fashioned, Prometheus "stops before Pandora's image" and addresses to it an impassioned hymn of praise: "And you, Pandora, sacred vessel of all gifts that are delightful under the broad sky, on the infinite earth—all that which has ever revived me with joyful feelings, which has poured relief on me in the cool of the shadow . . . all that which I have ever tasted as a pure radiance of heaven and a calm pleasure of the soul—all this, all this—my Pandora." [12] After having come to life, she remains her father's favorite daughter; but she is far from being deified. Rather she is a lovely, innocent, and wonderfully comprehending girl to whom her father confides the secrets of life and death—secrets that may be summed up in the Greek phrase ἔρωτος δὲ αἰτία θάνατος, "the cause of love, however, is death." When her sister, Myra, has died of a fever in her arms, the horror-stricken Pandora learns that all the pleasures and sorrows she has known before she saw death face to face—the beauty of the sun and the moon, the joyful dance, the kisses of her playmates, thirst and fatigue, the grief over a lost sheep, the pain of a wounded foot [13]— will be both ended and fulfilled in one ultimate experience. And when she hears that she cannot die at once and asks, "And after death?" she is told:

> *Wenn alles—Begier und Freud' und Schmerz—*
> *Im stürmenden Genuss sich aufgelös't,*
> *Dann sich erquickt in Wonneschlaf—*
> *Dann lebst du auf, auf's jüngste wieder auf,*
> *Von neuem zu fürchten, zu hoffen, zu begehren.* [14]

---

[12] Goethe, *Prometheus*, lines 173 ff.

[13] The incidents referred to in the text have attracted the attention of modern illustrators. In *Prometheus, dramatisches Fragment von Goethe* (Marées-Gesellschaft, J. Meier-Graefe, ed., Munich, 1920, illustrated by Felix Meseck), one etching shows Prometheus putting the final touches to the face of the statue that is to become Pandora (p. 6); a second, Myra dying in Pandora's arms (p. 41); a third, Pandora with a lamb and a sheep (p. 43); and a fourth, Prometheus extracting the thorn from Pandora's foot (p. 47). *Goethe, Prométhée, Traduction par André Gide*, Paris, 1950 (but finished, according to the colophon, in 1951), is illustrated with lithographs by

Henry Moore, among which we find the following Pandora scenes: Prometheus and Athena looking at Pandora's statue (p. 23); Pandora holding the dying Myra in her arms (p. 45); Pandora alone amidst a group of embryonic figures perforated by the holes without which Henry Moore figures would not be Henry Moore's (p. 51).

[14] Goethe, *Prometheus*, lines 419 ff.:

> *When all of this—desire and joy and*
> *   pain—*
> *Has melted and dissolved in stormy rapture*
> *And then refreshed itself in blissful sleep,*
> *You will revive, revive to fullest youth,*
> *To fear, to hope and to desire once more.*

Exactly fifty years later, when Goethe immortalized the end of his last passion—the half-reciprocated passion of a man of seventy-four for a girl of nineteen—in his *Trilogie der Leidenschaft,* Pandora had assumed an entirely different significance. Evoked in the concluding stanza of the "Marienbader Elegie" (the very heart of the *Trilogie*), she symbolizes a transcendent bliss fated to be withdrawn from him who has experienced it:

> *Mir ist das All, ich bin mir selbst verloren,*
> *Der ich noch erst den Göttern Liebling war;*
> *Sie prüften mich, verliehen mir Pandoren,*
> *So reich an Gütern, reicher an Gefahr;*
> *Sie drängten mich zum gabesel'gen Munde,*
> *Sie trennen mich und richten mich zu Grunde.*[15]

By a strange coincidence this transformation of Pandora, the radiant child, into Pandora, the symbol of a renunciation enforced by fate, can be traced back, it seems, to a chance encounter between Goethe and the mother of the very girl to whom we owe the *Trilogie der Leidenschaft,* Ulrike von Levetzow. In the summer of 1806, when Ulrike was a baby of two, Goethe met her mother, Amalia, at Karlsbad. As we learn from his diary, he was sufficiently attracted by this then youthful lady to think and speak of her, in a semifacetious way, as a reincarnation of the same mythical entity whom he was to conjure up, in deadly seriousness, when tearing himself away from her daughter: he privately nicknamed her "Pandora," and when she left Karlsbad, apparently in somewhat hurried fashion, the diary records this event as "Pandora's flight" ("Flucht der Pandora").[16] It was apparently by the tiny spark of this ephemeral relationship that Goethe's imagination was set ablaze with a multitude of new ideas and images that were to take shape in the play known to posterity as his *Pandora:* and chief among these new

---

[15] Goethe, *Elegie,* last stanza:
  To me all things are lost, to me myself,
  Who lately was the darling of the gods.
  The gods did try me, granted me Pandora,
  In goods so rich, in perils richer still.
  They urged me toward the mouth prepared to give;
  They keep me from her, and they ruin me.

[16] *Goethes Tagebücher,* III, Weimar, 1889, p. 150 (July 31, 1806); the other reference, reading "Frau von Levetzow (Pandora)," *ibidem,* p. 147 (July 27, 1806). Cf. Viëtor, *op. cit.,* p. 272; U. von Wilamowitz-Möllendorff, "Goethes Pandora," *Goethe Jahrbuch,* XIX, 1898, Appendix, pp. 1 * ff., particularly p. 6 *.

ideas and images was that of a Pandora relinquishing her lover after a period of perfect happiness and leaving behind her a sense of bereavement tempered only by the hope for her return.

When Goethe, in the fall of 1807, began to write this play, he entitled it *Pandorens Wiederkunft*. It was to begin, long after Pandora's departure from earth, with a nocturnal vigil filled with reminiscences and expectations, and it was to culminate in her triumphant return with the sun of a new day. It is significant, however, that this plan was never carried out—and, we may venture to say, could never have been carried out—in its entirety. On June 15, 1808, the first act, entitled *Pandorens Wiederkunft bis zum Abschied der Eos* ("Pandora's Return up to the Leave-taking of Dawn"), went to the printers,[17] but Goethe's brief outline of the ensuing events[18] was never elaborated. In retrospect he could say that his *Pandora*—that is, the torso published in 1808—expresses the same "sad feeling of deprivation" ("das schmerzliche Gefühl der Entbehrung") as does his novel, the *Wahlverwandtschaften*,[19] which was begun precisely at the moment when the completion of the Pandora play was abandoned. And when this play, as far as it existed, was performed on the stage, the perceptive Rahel Levin remarked that it had left her in a mood akin to dejection: "As in a flash I understood what it means to be old; I grew old then and there; old age, too, comes of a sudden."[20]

That this "sad feeling of deprivation," this sense of having grown old, had been predominant in Goethe's mind from the beginning (regardless of his unrealized and unrealizable intention to append to the "Pandora Lost" a "Pandora Regained")[21] is evident from the very first line of the play, which, as in a fugue, states the theme or "subject" of the entire composition: "Kindheit und Jugend, allzuglücklich preis' ich sie," "Childhood and youth, as all too happy these I praise." This line is spoken by Epimetheus; and he, a sec-

[17] *Goethes Tagebücher*, III, p. 347.
[18] *Goethes Werke*, L, Weimar, 1900, pp. 456 ff. The outline was written on May 18, 1808.
[19] Wilamowitz-Möllendorff, "Goethes Pandora," p. 17 *, n. 1.
[20] Quoted by Viëtor, *op. cit.*, p. 201.
[21] Yet a completion of Goethe's play, based on his outline of May 18, 1808, was attempted (with the same measure of success that attended the efforts to finish Schubert's "Unfinished" Symphony) by a well-known art historian: *Goethes Pandora mit einem Schluss von Franz Wickhoff und sechs Holzschnitten von Erwin Lang*, Vienna, 1932. None of the rather mediocre woodcuts shows Pandora herself.

ondary figure in Calderón's *Estatua de Prometeo* and entirely absent from Voltaire's *Pandore,* is the central character of Goethe's play as it stands. In it, Prometheus, the hero of Goethe's own youth, is no longer the godlike creator and liberator of mankind but a sober-minded utilitarian. He is "der Thätige," [22] the man of action whose life fulfills itself in the conquest of nature and the establishment of social order: his very torch, instead of transmitting the spark of life to human breasts, serves only to "anticipate the morning star" so that "manly work" may begin before daybreak. Epimetheus, on the other hand, is no longer the "stupid man who learns too late," [23] but a grand and moving figure. Elevated to the plane of what the ancients extolled as the *vita contemplativa,* he is the thinker as opposed to the doer; the solitary, imaginative dreamer, for whom the morning star appears too early rather than too late ("I fear the rooster's crowing as the morning star's / Precocious twinkle; would it were forever night"), [24] as opposed to the rationalist; he is, above all, endowed with a capacity for suffering [25] that enables him to desire, to enjoy, to forsake, to bemoan, and to desire again.

In the life of Goethe's Prometheus, woman has no place; the origin of his violent son, Phileros, is never accounted for, an omission deplored by certain critics [26] but, in our opinion, intentional and significant. He and his blacksmiths, shepherds, and warriors live in caves or Cyclopic masonry, "rough and crude, without any symmetry." Epimetheus, however, lives in a simple but entirely civilized environment: his home is an "austere wooden building" in the style of the earliest temples, the columns of its porch protecting a covered couch, which is surrounded by similar dwellings and well-tended orchards. And his whole life is dominated by the influence of a Pandora no longer thought of as either a daughter of Prometheus or a creature

---

[22] Goethe, *Pandora,* lines 29, 218, 316, 1045.

[23] "Ein alberer und unvorsichtiger Pursch," to quote from Benjamin Hederich, *Gründliches Lexicon Mythologicum,* Leipzig, 1724, col. 826. Goethe, though ridiculing Hederich's "naïveté," made extensive use of this earliest scholarly mythological dictionary; see E. Grumach, *Goethe und die Antike: eine Sammlung,* Berlin, 1949 (a very useful compilation, the acquaintance with which we owe to Mr.

Kurt Wolff), II, pp. 687–689.

[24] *Ibidem,* lines 24 ff.

[25] *Ibidem,* line 315. Prometheus, with reference to Epimetheus as opposed to himself: "Du dauerst mich und doch belob' ich dein Geschick. / Zu dulden ist! Sei's thätig oder leidend auch."

[26] Wilamowitz-Möllendorff, "Goethes Pandora," p. 8 *.

of Hephaestus (a "deluding fable" emphatically rejected by Epimetheus himself),[27] but as a descendant of Uranus, an equal to Hera, and a sister of Zeus.[28]

Refused admission by Prometheus—even though he recognizes her beauty and her accomplishments and, unlike his son, never speaks of her in the disparaging terms of Hesiod [29]—she has been accepted by Epimetheus and has illumined his life with all those values for which the man of action has no time and no use. Her "mysterious dowry," the vase, has released, instead of evils, a galaxy of little stars changing into lovely, floating images that dissolve into nothingness when reached for by "terrestrial hands"; but Epimetheus has found the consummation of his longings in Pandora herself.[30]

As the curtain rises, she has long left the earth to return whence she had come ("to the all-gifted nothing could I give," says Epimetheus),[31] accompanied by one of their two daughters, Elpore (Hope), and leaving with him the other, Epimeleia (Thoughtful Care).[32] And Epimetheus has spent the rest of his life remembering her. In the play itself he remembers her in a soliloquy induced by an encounter with young Phileros that makes him doubly conscious of his own age; he remembers her in a dream; he remembers her in an unforgettable dialogue with Prometheus (where he even remembers how often he has remembered her before);[33] and the very intensity of this Platonic ἀνάμνησις enables him to feel that he possesses as an unchanging idea what he has lost as a transient reality: to Prometheus' compassionate "And so, alas, forever she departed," he answers, "And so forever she belongs to

---

[27] Goethe, *Pandora*, lines 600 f.

[28] *Ibidem*, lines 602 f.

[29] *Ibidem*, lines 471–480. Seeing, in his mad jealousy, Pandora's image in her daughter, Epimeleia, Phileros calls the mother "disastrous to the fathers, a torture to the sons" and "a dazzling deception interwoven with perdition by the gods"; he even imputes to her the Hesiodian κύνεος νόος ("ein hündisches Herz").

[30] *Ibidem*, lines 85–131.

[31] *Ibidem*, line 650: "Der Allbegabten wusst' ich nicht zu geben mehr."

[32] In classical mythology Epimetheus and Pandora were, we remember, considered the parents of Pyrrha (see n. 8, p. 7). According to a tradition already warped by a tendency toward allegorization, however, Epimetheus (Afterthought) produced two daughters who, like those in Goethe's play, are personifications rather than persons but bear entirely different connotations: Prophasis, viz., Excuse (Pindar, *Pythean Odes*, v, 26 f.; see Pauly-Wissowa, *op. cit.*, VI, col. 181), and Metameleia, viz., Repentance (Scholium to Pindar, *Pythean Odes*, v, 55; see Pauly-Wissowa, *op. cit.*, XV, col. 1325).

[33] Goethe, *Pandora*, lines 274–740.

me." [34] But at long last the time has come for her return, explicitly if non-committally promised by Elpore (this is the scene represented in Grüner's engraving, *fig. 43*), and positively if implicitly announced by Eos: "Soon from heaven / Both word and deed, bliss-giving, shall descend, / A gift unthought of, and undreamt before." [35] Prometheus, "not enjoying novelty," does not look forward to this gift; he believes that "mankind has all it needs for life on earth." But Eos, departing, gently rebukes him:

> *You, the Titans, made a great·beginning;*
> *But to lead to timeless good and beauty*
> *Is for the immortals; let them govern.*[36]

*

THUS ends Goethe's *Pandora*, unique in that the sharp contours of intelligible concepts are so much softened and blurred by the colored rays of subjective sentiment that the intuitable, or poetic, meaning of the play by far transcends its definable, or allegorical, significance. Yet Goethe did intend it and all its details to be invested with such a significance, though it is only natural that more specific inferences can be drawn from the brief, dry catchwords that constitute the outline of the second act than from the glowing verses of the first. And these inferences tend to show that, when it comes to allegorical interpretation, even so boldly innovatory a poet as Goethe was very much indebted to an exegetic tradition that can be traced back to late antiquity. Formulated at a time when the gods and heroes of Greece had lost their substantial reality and, like everything else, had to "signify" some abstract idea or principle, this exegetic tradition, preserved by medieval scholarship, was vigorously revived in the Renaissance.[37] And though it may be "völlig wertlos" [38] to those who want to know what Pandora—or, for that matter, any other mythological character—really was in pre-Socratic or even pre-Hesiod-

---

[34] *Ibidem*, line 653 f.
[35] *Ibidem*, lines 1058–1060.
[36] *Ibidem*, lines 1061–end.
[37] It should be noted that Caelius Rhodiginus cites Tzetzes' interpretation of Pandora in 1517 (cf. below, p. 130) and that Henri Es-

tienne (quoted above, p. 65) alludes to it in 1566. As early as 1537, Trincavelli had published at Venice a Hesiod edition including all the scholia.
[38] Oldfather, in Pauly-Wissowa, *op. cit.*, XVIII, 3, col. 544.

ian religion, it cannot be neglected by those who want to know what Pandora—or, for that matter, any other mythological character—happened to become in modern art and literature.

To return, then, to the unwritten second act of Goethe's *Pandora*. It would have opened, after an introductory bacchanal of fishermen and wine-growers, with the descent from heaven of the "gift" announced by Eos at the end of the first act. This "gift" is a mysterious shrine or chest (Κυπσέλη) the advent of which is acclaimed by Phileros, Epimeleia, and Epimetheus, whereas Prometheus, supported by the warriors, insists on its destruction, and the blacksmiths propose to dismantle it for professional examination. Then, however, Pandora herself appears, "paralyzing the violent," winning over the peaceable, and bringing with her "happiness and comfort" ("Glück und Bequemlichkeit"). And under the aegis of "Beauty" ("Schönheit") there begins a reign of piety and tranquillity described—with a truly Goethean fusion of the Scriptural and the Hellenic—as "Sabbath" and "Moria," the latter term denoting Athena's sacred olive tree at Athens. Near the end, the mysterious Κυπσέλη—a Pandora's box in reverse, so to speak— "opens itself up" and discloses, instead of untold evils, a "Temple," "Sitting Daemons," [39] "Science," and "Art." Epimetheus, rejuvenated, soars to heaven together with Pandora; priests give their blessing; and after a final chorus "Elpore thraseia" (that is, Elpore transfigured in the image of Thucydides' ἐλπὶς θρασεῖα, Confident Hope) bids farewell to the spectators.

The words "Science" and "Art" have a familiar ring: we know them from Calderón, who, we recall, conceives of Pandora as a Minerva reincarnate, and, consequently, credits her with propagating *artes y ciencias* among mankind. Goethe knew and admired Calderón [40] and possibly remembered the *Estatua de Prometeo* when sketching the finale of his own *Pandora*. However, the idea that Pandora, "all-gifted" and taught by Pallas Athene, typifies the arts—which, by Greek standards, comprise what we would call the crafts and skills as well as the applied sciences, shipbuilding and agriculture

---

[39] The English language fortunately permits a distinction in spelling between the Greek δαίμων (a spirit or genius, nearly always of benevolent character) and the Christian *demon*.

[40] K. Wolf, "Goethe und Calderón," *Goethe Jahrbuch*, XXXIV, 1913, pp. 118 ff.; F. Strich, *Goethe und die Weltliteratur*, Bern, 1946, pp. 159 ff.

as well as rhetoric—is very much older than Calderón. It was, in fact, conceived and elaborated in classical antiquity itself and very much alive (though not always endorsed) in Goethe's own time.[41]

"If Jupiter orders Vulcan to fashion Pandora," says Manuel Moschopoulos, the learned Byzantine scholiast of the early fourteenth century, "this means that she is thought of as an allegorical representation of the arts (εἰς τὰς τέχνας ἀλληγορουμένην)," and he goes on to explain how the co-operation of Minerva symbolizes the fact that art cannot operate without reason; how the gifts of Venus typify the embellishment of its products with a pleasing appearance; how the dubious contributions of Mercury represent the persuasive but often misleading artifices of dialectics and oratory; and how the ministrations of the Horae indicate the temporal and seasonal changes that are of such importance for the practice of the arts.[42]

One and one-half centuries before Moschopoulos, the even more erudite Johannes Tzetzes had unearthed a passage of Aeschylus (evidently the Alexandrian grammarian rather than the great tragedian) according to which Pandora, compounded of water and earth with the aid of fire (Hephaestus), is not a woman but represents "the arts, contingent upon the discovery of fire, by means of which lumber was cut from the earth and ships were built and launched upon the sea; so that earth and water were jointly placed at the disposal of men who, on those earth-born ships, travel about the oceanic waters and engage in commerce."[43] And in two other passages, astonishingly prophetic of Goethe's "Glück und Bequemlichkeit, die sie [Pandora] bringt," the same Tzetzes restates this notion within its proper framework, that evolutionistic theory about the origins of human civilization which played such an important part in Greek and Roman writing and was to become one of the strongest forces in postmedieval thought. Prometheus' theft, he says, means

[41] See, e.g., Hederich, *op. cit.*, cols. 1495 f.: "wie aber solche Pandora die aller erste Frau gewesen seyn soll, also deuten sie einige nicht so ganz uneben auf die *Euam*, unser aller Mutter. Denn dass einige die Kunst, andere das τὸ ἄλογον τῆς ψυχῆς u. d. gl. unter ihr verstehen, sind gezwungene Subtilitaeten."

[42] Moschopoulos, to *Works and Days*, 60 (Gaisford, *op. cit.*, p. 72 f.).

[43] Tzetzes, to *Works and Days*, 60 (Gaisford, p. 72). Caelius Rhodiginus, *loc. cit.*, refers to Tzetzes as follows: "Ioannes tamen grammaticus artium inventionem Pandorae nomine accipiendam putat. Aquam vero subactam dici et terram ob navigationem excogitatam; aut per exochen quandam agricolationem intelligamus, a qua profluunt omnia quibus alimur."

that mankind had learned the use of fire and was thus able to develop the arts that make life more agreeable and luxurious, "thereby charming us into submission to more feminine habits, which is what the poet calls the formation of woman"; then, he continues, "we acquired all kinds of artifices, sophistication, the supererogatory invention of all the other arts, and the readjustment of a hard and simple life to softer and more effeminate standards; all of which may be designated as 'the woman Pandora,' as a 'thick-woven carpet,' or by a thousand other names." [44] And (with special reference to the pithos incident): "The opulent way of life resulting from the arts spread and divulged, or brought to light, that which had been unknown or difficult of access before and made it known and manifest to all." [45]

This *kulturgeschichtliche* or technological interpretation of the Pandora myth rivaled, and occasionally interpenetrated with, others: moralistic, psychological, and, ultimately, metaphysical. The moralistic approach is represented by Plutarch and Porphyry. According to Plutarch, Hesiod used the name of Zeus as a synonym for the power of Fortune (Τύχη), so that his gifts to Pandora (Διὸς δῶρα) signify such external blessings as wealth, successful marriage, and high office—in short, all those "outward things (τὰ ἐκτός) the possession of which is unprofitable to him who does not know how to make good use of them." [46] According to Porphyry, Pandora is a personification of Pleasure ('Ηδονή) in the unfavorable sense with which this concept had been invested by Xenophon's tale of the Choice of Hercules. [47]

Such later Neoplatonists as Proclus and Olympiodorus, on the other hand, identified her with that "irrational life force" (ἄλογος ζωὴ σωματική)

<hr>

[44] Tzetzes, to *Works and Days*, 42 (Gaisford, *op. cit.*, p. 59). For classical speculation on the primitive state of mankind and its evolution into a more civilized state, see A. O. Lovejoy and G. Boas, *Primitivism and Related Ideas in Antiquity*, Baltimore, 1935, *passim*; cf. also E. Panofsky, *Studies in Iconology*, New York, 1939, pp. 38 ff.

[45] Tzetzes, to *Works and Days*, 95 (Gaisford, *op. cit.*, p. 87).

[46] Plutarch, *Moralia*, 23, E. F. ("How the Young Man Should Study Poetry," referred to in Pauly-Wissowa, *op. cit.*, XVIII, 3, col. 544). Plutarch's interpretation is mentioned by Elton, *op. cit.*, p. 12, as having been approved by the great philologist Daniel Heinsius.

[47] Porphyrius, *De antro Nympharum*, XXX, L. Holsten, ed., Utrecht, 1765, p. 27 (referred to in Pauly-Wissowa, *ibidem*, with the somewhat misleading addition that Tzetzes had held a similar view): καὶ παρ' 'Ησιόδῳ ὁ μέν τις νοεῖται πίθος δεδεμένος, ὃν λύει ἡ ἡδονή, καὶ εἰς πάντα διασκεδάννυσιν, μόνης ἐλπίδος μενούσης. ἐν οἷς γὰρ ἡ φαύλη ψυχὴ σκιδαμένη περὶ ὕλην τάξεως διαμαρτάνει . . .

or "irrational soul" (ἄλογος ψυχή, τὸ ἄλογον τῆς ψυχῆς) which links the "rational soul" to the body, and this interpretation, too, was known throughout the eighteenth century.[48]

Here, then, she symbolizes a principle that subjects us to physical needs and to the disturbing influence of the senses,[49] but, for this very reason, not only endows our very bodies with a share in beauty,[50] but also (and in this respect the Neoplatonic exegesis has absorbed the notions transmitted by Tzetzes and Moschopoulos) enables us to practice the arts and crafts: "There is some artistic ability in the feminine, irrational part of the soul because the imagination is skillful and capable in forming images; and this may well be referred to as something taught by Minerva."[51]

While this kind of interpretation—faintly echoed, perhaps, in Fulgentius' "quod anima munus sit omnium generale"[52]—may be described as metaphysics applied to psychology, Plotinus, the father of Neoplatonism, looks upon Pandora from the point of view of metaphysics pure and simple. According to him, her formation by Prometheus and her subsequent perfection by all the gods, especially Venus and the Graces, mean that the visible universe, resplendent with the "lights" and "souls" imparted to it from the outset by divine providence (προμήθεια), is further embellished with additional ornaments, imparted to it by countless other spiritual forces (called, in Plotinian terminology, "gods" and "minds").[53] The myth of Pandora, then, illustrates the basic tenet of Neoplatonism that the material world is infused and, as it were, illumined by that intelligible beauty which emanates from God but on its descent into the world of matter is enriched and diversified

---

[48] See the following note.

[49] Olympiodorus, *Comm. in Platonis Gorgiam,* XLVII, 5–7 (*Olympiodori Philosophi in Platonis Gorgiam commentarii,* W. Norvin, ed., Leipzig, 1936, p. 233). According to Olympiodorus (probably active at Alexandria in the sixth century A.D.), the bestowal of gifts upon Pandora signifies the influence of the celestial bodies upon the lower world in general and the irrational soul in particular. Epimetheus (Man) is interpreted as the recipient and guardian of the irrational soul whereas Prometheus is the guardian of the rational soul as symbolized by fire. Olympiodorus' interpretation is referred to, e.g., by Hederich

(see n. 41, p. 130) and Elton, *op. cit.,* p. 12.

[50] Proclus, to *Works and Days,* 63 (Gaisford, *op. cit.,* p. 74).

[51] Proclus, to *Works and Days,* 64 (Gaisford, *op. cit.,* pp. 74 f.).

[52] See above, p. 9.

[53] Plotinus, *Enneads,* IV, 3, 14: τούτων δὴ γινομένων φῶτα πολλὰ ὁ κόσμος οὗτος ἔχων καὶ καταυγαζόμενος ψυχαῖς ἐπικοσμεῖται ἐπὶ τοῖς προτέροις ἄλλους κόσμους ἄλλον παρ' ἄλλου κομιζόμενος, παρά τε θεῶν ἐκείνων παρά τε νῶν τῶν ἄλλων ψυχὰς διδόντων· οἷον εἰκὸς καὶ τὸν μῦθον αἰνίττεσθαι, ὡς πλάσαντος τοῦ Προμηθέως τὴν γυναῖκα ἐπεκόσμησαν αὐτὴν καὶ οἱ ἄλλοι θεοί, καὶ Ἀφροδίτην τι δοῦναι καὶ Χάρ-

by intermediary agencies—that, as Ficino expresses it in his commentary upon the very passage here under discussion, "in natural things there are inherent, not only animal forces but also endowments intelligible and divine." [54]

It was in 1805—not, as he himself imagined at a much later date, as a youth of fifteen or sixteen—that Goethe became familiar with Plotinus' *Enneads*.[55] It was one of his fundamental experiences, so fundamental that he at once proceeded to translate a number of chapters into German and subsequently inserted these translations into *Wilhelm Meisters Wanderjahre*; and it has rightly been said that his Pandora play, conceived and executed under the fresh impact of this experience, is thoroughly imbued with the Plotinian doctrine of beauty.[56] Were it permissible to define the indefinable, the nearest approximation to a definition of what Goethe's Pandora ultimately "signifies" might be: the principle of cosmic beauty as conceived by Plotinus; the "Abglanz jenes Urlichts droben, / Das unsichtbar alle Welt erleuchtet";[57] or—which, from the Neoplatonic point of view, amounts to the same thing—the ideated form (εἶδος) that irradiates matter.[58] On the occasion of her final

---

ιτας καὶ ἄλλον ἄλλο δῶρον καὶ ὀνομάσαι ἐκ τοῦ δώρου καὶ πάντων τῶν δεδωκότων. πάντες γὰρ τούτῳ ἔδοσαν τῷ πλάσματι παρὰ προμηθείας τινὸς γενομένῳ.

For the most recent translation—rather, a paraphrase—of this somewhat difficult passage, cf. V. Cilento, *Plotino, Enneadi, prima versione integra e commentario critico*, Bari, 1947 ff., II, pp. 197 f. We have assumed, with Cilento and others, that the ψυχαῖς in the first sentence belongs to καταυγαζόμενος and not, as supposed by some, to ἐπικοσμεῖται. For the problem presented by the following sentence beginning with ὁ δὲ Προμηθεύς, see p. 135.

[54] Marsilio Ficino, *Opera omnia*, Basel, 1576, II, p. 1738.

[55] See M. Wundt, "Plotin und die Romantik," *Neue Jahrbücher für das klassische Altertum, Geschichte und deutsche Literatur*, XXXVI, 1915, p. 649 ff.; idem, "Noch einmal Goethe und Plotin," *ibidem*, XLI, 1918, pp. 140 f.; furthermore, H. F. Mühle, "Goethe und Plotinos," *Germanisch-Romanische Monatsschrift*, VII, 1915-19, pp. 45 ff., F. Koch, *Goethe und Plotin*, Leipzig, 1925; Viëtor, *op. cit.*, pp. 426 ff. From the passages conveniently collected

in Grumach, *op. cit.*, II, pp. 815 ff., it is quite evident that it was Friedrich August Wolf and not, as assumed by Wundt, Georg Friedrich Creuzer who called Goethe's attention to Plotinus and, in August, 1805, supplied him with an edition of the Greek original. Creuzer did not approach Goethe in writing until 1806 and did not meet him in person until 1815 (Grumach, II, p. 706). Goethe's reference to his early interest in Plotinus is found in a passage inserted, at a very late date, into the Sixth Book of his autobiography, *Dichtung und Wahrheit* (*Goethes Werke*, XXVII, Weimar, 1889, p. 382; Grumach, p. 815), which contains many "reprojections" of this kind.

[56] Wilamowitz-Möllendorff, *op. cit.*, and particularly, Cassirer, *op. cit.* See also Viëtor, *op. cit.*, pp. 198 ff., with special reference to Epimetheus' hymn quoted in n. 59, p. 134.

[57] From Goethe's *Vorspiel zur Eröffnung des Weimarer Theaters*, 1807 (the same year in which *Pandora* was conceived and partly written), quoted by Viëtor, *op. cit.*, p. 199.

[58] This principle is almost literally stated by Epimetheus in Goethe, *Pandora*, line 676: "Und einzig veredelt die Form den Gehalt."

theophany, we remember, the qualities of the blissful state inaugurated by her reappearance are condensed into the single word "Schönheit," and when Epimetheus attempts to describe her essence to his brother, falling from iambic trimeters into a hymn of rhymed stanzas, he summarizes, as it were, the content of the fifth *Ennead,* emanation, re-emanation, and all.[59]

In adding the adjective "cosmic" to "beauty," we have tacitly assumed that Goethe knew the specific passage in which Plotinus deals with the Pandora myth, and this tacit assumption can be borne out, we think, on philological grounds. As we know by Goethe's own testimony, he read the *Enneads* in a Latin translation, consulting the Greek original only "for revision"; and this translation can have been only Ficino's.[60] In his rendering of the critical passage, now, Ficino had not only followed a recension, substituting Epimetheus for Prometheus, which—though accepted by competent scholars up to our day—is clearly aberrant, but he also committed a palpable mistake, not to be challenged until 1835, of his own. And it would seem that both these

[59] Goethe, *Pandora,* lines 655–678:

Der Seligkeit Fülle die hab' ich empfunden!
Die Schönheit besass ich, sie hat mich gebunden;
Im Frühlingsgefolge trat herrlich sie an.
Sie erkannt' ich, sie ergriff ich, da war es gethan!
Wie Nebel zerstiebte trübsinniger Wahn,
Sie zog mich zur Erd' ab, zum Himmel hinan.

Du suchest nach Worten sie würdig zu loben,
Du willst sie erhöhen, sie wandelt schon oben.
Vergleich' ihr das Beste; du hältst es für schlecht.
Sie spricht, du besinnst dich; doch hat sie schon Recht.
Du stemmst dich entgegen; sie gewinnt das Gefecht.
Du schwankst ihr zu dienen, und bist schon ihr Knecht.

Das Gute, das Liebe, das mag sie erwidern.
Was hilft hohes Ansehn? Sie wird es erniedern.
Sie stellt sich an's Ziel hin, beflügelt den Lauf;
Vertritt sie den Weg dir, gleich hält sie dich auf.
Du willst ein Gebot thun, sie treibt dich hinauf,
Gibst Reichthum und Weisheit und alles in den Kauf.

Sie steiget hernieder in tausend Gebilden,
Sie schwebet auf Wassern, sie schreitet auf Gefilden,
Nach heiligen Massen erglänzt sie und schallt,
Und einzig veredelt die Form den Gehalt,
Verleiht ihm, verleiht sich die höchste Gewalt,
Mir erschien sie in Jugend-, in Frauen-Gestalt.

[60] Goethe, *Dichtung und Wahrheit, loc. cit.:* "ich suchte mich dem Text durch die lateinische Uebersetzung zu nähern." See also Goethe's letters to F. A. Wolf of August 29, 1805, and Karl Friedrich Zelter of September 1, 1805 (Grumach, *op. cit.,* II, pp. 816 and 817 f.) : "denn obgleich der Uebersetzer seinen Autor, im ganzen und einzelnen, recht wohl verstanden haben mag, so scheinen doch mehrere Stellen dunkel . . ." and: "Sie erhalten hierbey die Uebersetzung einer Uebersetzung; sobald ich sie nach dem Original revidieren kann, werden die Worte freylich ganz anders klingen." Goethe may have used the Salignac edition of 1540 or, more probably, the Basel edition of 1559. For several other cases in which Goethe demonstrably quoted from Ficino instead of Plotinus or even Plato, see P. O. Kristeller, *Il pensiero filosofico di Marsilio Ficino,* Florence, 1953, p. 110 (with ample references).

misapprehensions left their marks on Goethe's imagination—which, being Goethe's, turned the defects into virtues.

After having established the parallel between the supervening gifts of the gods to Pandora and the supervening embellishment of the visible universe, Plotinus continues as follows: ὁ δὲ Προμηθεὺς ἀποποιούμενος τὸ δῶρον αὐτοῦ τί ἂν σημαίνοι ἢ τὴν τοῦ ἐν νοητῷ μᾶλλον αἵρεσιν ἀμείνω εἶναι;, which means in English: "And if *Prometheus rejects the gift of it* [meaning the gift of the πλάσμα, statue, as perfected by the gods], what may this signify if not the fact that the choice of the intelligible is much better [*scil.*, than the choice of that which is perceptible by the senses]?" Ficino, however, translated this sentence as follows: "Quod autem Epimetheus ei [*scil.*, Pandorae] donum dederit nullum, quidnam aliud significat quam acceptionem electionemque doni intelligibilis esse praestantiorem?" "And if *Epimetheus never gave her any gift*, what does this signify if not that the acceptance and choice of an intelligible boon is to be preferred?" [61]

[61] *Plotini opera Marsilio Ficino interprete*, Florence, 1492, fol. bb IIII r. The difficulty about the passage is that only three manuscripts of the *Enneads* (among them, however, the venerable Laurentianus 87, 3, referred to as "A" in Plotinus philology) have Προμηθεύς while all the others have 'Επιμηθεύς; see Cilento, *op. cit.*, II, p. 497, and I, p. 262 ff. The authorities are divided; but it can hardly be questioned that only Προμηθεύς makes sense. There is no evidence in any classical source for the notion that Epimetheus ever rejected Pandora or that he was a champion of the νοητόν; Himerius, *Oratio* LXVIII (*Himerii Declamationes et orationes*, A. Colonna, ed., Rome, 1951, p. 241), adduced by Creuzer (*Plotini opera omnia*, F. Creuzer, ed., Oxford, 1835, II, p. 710, III, pp. 213 f.) and others in this connection, says only that, according to Protagoras, Zeus, after having made all men alike, ordered two daemons, Prometheus and Epimetheus, to aid Nature by putting into them, first, mind and perception, second, strength and speed. Moreover, the direct continuation of the controversial Plotinus passage —beginning with δέδεται and saying that the creator remains "bound" to his creature, a situation symbolized by Prometheus' being fettered to Mount Caucasus—clearly refers to him and not to his brother. If many reputable scholars, from Ficino to Cilento, decided for the 'Επιμηθεύς reading, they may have been swayed by the αὐτοῦ (only arbitrarily corrected into αὐτῶν in some editions), which they took to refer to Προμηθεύς: it seemed nonsensical that Prometheus should have refused to accept a gift from himself. This difficulty can be resolved, however, by an ingenious suggestion of our friend Professor Cherniss, who proposes to interpret the bothersome αὐτοῦ, not as a subjective genitive governed by Προμηθεύς, but as an objective genitive referring back to πλάσματι: Prometheus "refused the gift of it," that is to say, the gift of the statue fashioned by himself but in the meantime manipulated and transformed by his enemies, the gods. Ficino's translation of ἀποποιούμενος τὸ δῶρον αὐτοῦ as "ei donum dederit nullum" (apparently a desperate attempt to avoid the idea of Epimetheus' "rejecting" Pandora) is, of course, untenable from any philological point of view and was rightly corrected by Creuzer, *loc. cit.*, into "donum eius rejecit." In his commentary on *Enneads*, IV, 3, 14 (*Opera omnia*, II, col. 1738), Ficino limits himself to paraphrasing the analogies that link Prometheus to providence, the statues to the natural things, the clay used for the fashioning of the statues to prime matter, and the binding of Prometheus

In the phrase "ei donum dederit nullum," this indefensible rendering anticipates the wistful line of Goethe's Epimetheus: "To the all-gifted nothing could I give." And when—with a logic appealing to poets rather than philosophers—Ficino's translation seems to connect the supposed Epimetheus' alleged "disinclination to give" with his readiness to "accept and choose the *donum intelligibile*" in preference to more tangible values, and thereby transforms the foolish brother into the wiser one, this misinterpretation of a questionable reading, coming to Goethe's attention at what may be called the providential moment, may well have operated in his mind as does the little piece of string that, suspended in the solution of a crystallizable substance, sets off and promotes the process of crystallization. Ascribing to Epimetheus that superior wisdom which withdraws from the world of sensory perception and practical activity into a world of dreams and ideas, Ficino's version of Plotinus' Pandora passage would seem to have initiated the "crystallization" of the self-revelatory image that was to take shape in the resigned, "contemplative" Epimetheus of Goethe's play.

The Neoplatonic philosophy, so vulnerable from every epistemological and scientific point of view, has had, and in a manner still has, an undying fascination for the poetic mind. Plotinus' concept of beauty was wide enough to accommodate the rationalistic identification of Pandora with the arts and sciences; yet it was deep enough to absorb the emotional experiences of the aging Goethe. To discover in his *Pandora* not only the influence of Plotinus —and, for that matter, Ficino—but also the effect of less exalted yet equally ancient traditions adds little to our understanding of it; but it does show that even the greatest of mortals is not like God, who created something out of nothing, but has to "manipulate some material that existed before."

---

to the role of providence in the operations of nature in which, he adds, "Epimetheus, viz., rashness [*temeritas*], has no place." This interpretation, based on the fact that Epimetheus acts first and thinks afterward, is, needless to say, at variance with Ficino's own translation of the Plotinus passage. Pandora is not mentioned in his commentary.

Addenda

Addenda

(1) To pp. 68 f. ("Pandora's Box" as a common noun denoting a collection of things or ideas)

In eighteenth-century New England the term "Pandora's Box" seems to have been applied to a receptacle containing several medical instruments, perhaps not unlike the proverbial "little black bag" of the country doctor. In 1721 "inoculators" were enjoined to "be compleatly armed with Incision-Lancet, Pandora's Box, Nut-Shell and Fillet." [1]

(2) To pp. 67, 79–84 (Pandora as a malevolent water nymph)

In the Tenth Canto of his much-praised and much-maligned *Adone* (first published in 1623), Giovanni Battista Marino has a description of Pandora so characteristic of a "Mannerist" mind conversant with classical as well as Italian and French sources and given to reckless accumulation of conflicting ideas and metaphors that it is worth quoting. Alternately designating the fateful vessel as "vase" (*vase, vaso*), "urn" (*urna*), and even "box" (*bossolo*), Marino conflates the version of Hesiod with that of Babrius—making the virtues escape while the evils remain "at the bottom"—and, from a purely visual point of view, portrays Pandora much as she appears in Bonasone's engraving (*fig. 32*).

Guided by Venus and Mercury, Adonis enters the sphere of the moon, where he approaches the "Cave of Nature," its entrance guarded by two seated goddesses, "Felicità" on the right and "Miseria" on the left. Each of these goddesses superintends, as it were, a river; but these are very different in quality as well as quantity. The crystal-clear but somewhat scanty waters of the "river of bliss" are distilled, drop by drop, from an alembic held by

[1] Sir William A. Craigie and James R. Hulbert, eds., *A Dictionary of American Eng-* *lish on Historical Principles*, III, Chicago, 1942, p. 1676.

"Felicità." The copious but muddy waters of the "river of misery," however, come from a very different source: [2]

L'altro ruscel, che men purgato e chiaro
Passa da manca, è tutto di veleno,
Viè più che fiel, viè più ch'assenzio amaro,
E sol pianti e sciagure accoglie in seno.
Vedi colei che 'l vaso onde volaro
Le compagne d'Astrea tutto n' ha pieno,
E con prodiga man sovra i mortali
Sparge quanti mai fur malori e mali.

Pandora è quella; il bossolo di Giove
Folle audacia ad aprir le persuase.
Fuggì lo stuol de le virtuti altrove,
Le disgrazie restaro in fondo al vase.
Sol la Speranza in cima a l'orlo, dove
Sempre accompagna i miseri, rimase;
Ed è quella colà vestita a verde,
Che'n Ciel non entra, e nell'entrar si perde.

Or vedi come fuor de l'ampia bocca
De l'urna rea ch'ogni difetto asconde
In larga vena scaturisce e fiocca
Il sozzo umor di quelle perfid'onde.
De l'altro fiume onde piacer trabocca,

[2] Stanzas 73-76:

The other river, running on the left,
Less clear and limpid, is all poisonous;
More bitter than both gall and wormwood, it
Holds nothing but laments and misery.
And I saw her who holds the vase, still full,
Whence the companions of Astraea [viz., the Virtues] fled
While she with spendthrift hand disperses all
The evils and disasters among men.

She is Pandora whom mad imprudence
Persuaded to unseal the box [bossolo] of Jove.

Out flew the virtues, bound for other realms,
While in the vessel's [vase] base the evils stayed;
Hope only lingered on the rim above,
Where she attends our miseries forever.
Clad in green garb, she does not enter heaven,
For if she does, she ceases to exist.

From the wide mouth of the accursèd urn [urna]
That hides all evils I saw flow and gush
The ugly liquid of that treacherous stream
Which carries waters much more plentiful

Questo in copia maggior l'acque diffonde,
Perchè in quel nido di tormenti e guai
Sempre l'amaro è più che'l dolce assai.

Vedi morte, penuria, e guerra e peste,
Vecchiezza e povertà con bassa fronte,
Pena, angoscia, fatica, afflitte e meste
Figlie appo lei d'Averno e d'Acheronte.
Ve' l'empia Ingratitudine tra queste,
Prima d'ogni altro mal radice e fonte,
E tutte uscite son del vaso immondo
Per infestar, per infettar il mondo.

(3) To p. 117, n. 2

PROFESSOR HENRI PEYRE kindly reminds us of the fact that a free translation of Le Sage's *La Boîte de Pandore* was published by Christoph Martin Wieland in 1779.[3] In a little preface Wieland himself emphasized the fact that he made several changes (the ideas of including Prometheus in the *dramatis personae*, of "relieving Mercury of his Harlequin's mask," and of infusing into the whole more *Sinn, Gestalt, und Rundung*) so that "what had started as a mere translation became *beinahe etwas ganz Neues.*"

Than does the second river, that of joy;
Which goes to show that in this vale of tears
More bitterness than sweetness is in store.

You see Death, Indigence, and War, and Plague,
Old Age, and Poverty with downcast face;

And, near to them Pain, Anguish, Weariness,
Sad brood of Acheron and of Avernus.
Among these dwells profane Ingratitude
First root and source of all the other wrongs;
And all had issued from that unclean vase [vaso]
In order to infest, infect, the world.

[3] *C. M. Wielands sämtliche Werke*, Leipzig, XXVIII, 1857, pp. 329 ff.

Addenda to the Second Edition

(4) To pp. 4–9

PANDORA IN ANTIQUITY. Exclusive authenticity has again been claimed for the Hesiodian version of the Pandora story (based on the premise that the fateful vessel contains evils exclusively, and presumably implying that Hope is either one of these evils or, at best, a kind of delusion) by O. Lendle, *Die "Pandorasage" bei Hesiod, Textkritische und motivgeschichtliche Untersuchungen*, Würzburg, 1957; and by K. Reinhardt, "Prometheus," *Eranos-Jahrbuch*, xxv, 1957, pp. 241 ff., particularly pp. 251–56 (cf. also *idem*, "Vorschläge zum neuen Aischylos," *Hermes*, LXXXV, pp. 16 f., 125 f.). Yet the problem posed by the two passages in Hesiod remains unresolved and is perhaps unresolvable. In his excellent essay, Reinhardt himself stresses the fact that the account in *Theogony* cannot be reconciled with that in *Works and Days*; and that his own answer to the question of the "truly original version" of the myth (*das Ursprüngliche*) can be no more than "*very* hypothetical" (italics his). In his review of our book (*Gnomon*, xxx, 1958, pp. 386 ff., particularly pp. 389 f.), O. Brendel also acknowledges the difficulties surrounding the original version of the myth but points out that the very presence of *Pandoras genesis* on the base of Phidias' *Parthenos* would seem to indicate the existence of an "optimistic" interpretation at least in fifth-century Athens.

The theory that Pandora was originally an earth goddess has been defended by G. Fink, *Pandora und Epimetheus; Mythologische Studien* (diss. Erlangen), 1958, in spite of having earlier been (we think, convincingly) refuted by E. Buschor, *Feldmäuse* (Sitzungsberichte der Bayerischen Akademie der Wissenschaften, Phil.-hist. Abtlg., I), 1937, pp. 22 ff. For Pandora in the satyric drama, see F. Brommer, *Satyrspiele,* 2nd ed., Berlin, 1959, pp. 52 ff. We owe these three references to Dr. Erika Simon.

(5) To p. 11, n. 22

BOCCACCIO'S "PANDORA HOMO." Boccaccio's curious description of Pandora as "a man" (*homo*) is discussed in an article we had overlooked; it was brought to our attention by Professor William S. Heckscher: G. Scarlata, "*De Pandora Homine* (Giov. Boccaccio—*Genealogia Deorum Gentilium*—IV–XLV)," *La Tradizione,* IV, 1931, fasc. II (March–April), pp. 3 ff. The author convincingly explains Boccaccio's surprising statement as a conflation of two distinct and factually unrelated sentences in Fulgentius' *Mythologiae:* "Prometheum aiunt hominem ex luto fecisse" and "denique [Prometheus] dicitur Pandoram formasse" (quoted above, p. 9, n. 16).

(6) To pp. 15–17

ERASMUS' SUBSTITUTION OF "PYXIS" FOR "DOLIUM" AND OF EPIMETHEUS FOR PANDORA. The liberties Erasmus had taken with the classical story were aptly criticized, at a comparatively early date, by Francisco Sánchez de las Brozas, professor at the University of Salamanca: *Francisci Sanctis Brocensis . . . Comment. in And. Alciati Emblemata,* Lyons (Rouille), 1573, p. 179. Commenting on the emblem *Simulacrum Spei* (our *fig. 12*), he writes: "Erasmus in adagio Malo accepto stultus sapit, narrat hanc fabulam, sed concise, et qui videatur innuere Epimetheum aperuisse pixidem (si pixis vocandum est vas illud, quod omnia mala continebat, et non dolium), cum ipsa Pandora in domo Epimethei repertum vas aperuit. Certe verba Hesiodi non indicant vas illud posse Latine dici pixidem ἀλλὰ γυνὴ χείρεσσι πίθου μέγα πῶμα ἀφελοῦσα. . . . Hoc est, Sed mulier manibus magnum operculum auferens, etc." ("Erasmus tells this fable in his adage 'The fool gets wise after having been hurt,' but only summarily, and he seems to suggest that it is Epimetheus who opens the box—if that vessel which contained all the evils can indeed be called 'box' instead of 'cask'—whereas it was

Pandora who opened the vessel when she had found it in Epimetheus' house. The words of Hesiod certainly do not indicate that this vessel can be called *pyxis* in Latin: ἀλλὰ γυνὴ χείρεσσι πίθου μέγα πῶμα ἀφελοῦσα. . . , which means, 'but the woman took off the big lid with her hands.' ")

(7) To pp. 20 f., *fig. 1*

Adriaen de Vries' "Psyche Carried to Heaven." A similar group by Adriaen de Vries, dated 1593 and differing from the Stockholm version (our *fig. 1*) in that Psyche is transported to heaven by Mercury rather than three Cupids, is preserved in the Louvre (No. 536). The iconography of the Stockholm version agrees, however, with that of an etching by Giuseppe Diamantini, nonsensically described as "Psyche with the Box of Pandora, Surrounded by Cupids" in "Supplement zu den Handbüchern der Kupferstichkunde," *Repertorium für Kunstwissenschaft*, v, 1882, p. 4 (brought to our attention by Professor Wolfgang Lotz).

(8) To pp. 21 f., *figs. 2, 3*

Psyche (?) in Two Engravings by a Follower of Marcantonio Raimondi. In *Gnomon*, xxx, 1958, p. 388, O. Brendel, believing that the women represented in these engravings are both asleep, concludes that neither of them can be identified with either Psyche or Pandora; he proposes instead to interpret the subjects of the two prints as (1) The Night Descending upon the Earth with a Vessel Full of Dreams; and (2) The Night Returning to the Heavens after the Vessel Has Been Emptied. But, quite apart from the fact that the rendering of the eyes makes it extremely difficult to decide whether they are indeed closed or only shadowed, there is, so far as we know, no evidence for a connection between the Night and Mercury; and certain it is that she, a goddess herself, did not depend on Mercury for transportation. Where she is not imagined as winged (Virgil, *Aeneid*, viii, 369) she has a chariot of her own: Euripides, *Ion*, 1150; Tibullus, *Carmina*, iii, 4, 17; Boccaccio, *Genealogia deorum*, i, 9, followed by all the Renaissance mythographers.

More attractive is a hypothesis proposed, *in litteris*, by M. Guy de Tervarent. He suggests that the two engravings might represent a contrast between two different mythological characters rather than two different moments from one and the same story: according to him, the print reproduced in our *fig. 2* would show Pandora brought to earth, whereas the print reproduced in our *fig. 3* would show Psyche conveyed to heaven. This interpretation would be concordant with the mythographical data insofar as the texts do describe Mercury as Pandora's escort on her way down, and as Psyche's escort on her way up. But it is hard to reconcile with the fact that, if the woman represented in the engraving *fig. 3* were Psyche, her vessel, containing as it would the "little bit of Proserpina's beauty," ought to be upright, sealed, and full (as in our *fig. 1*); whereas it is in fact inverted, open, and empty. We must, to quote Lessing, "accord its lawful rights to the modest *Non liquet.*"

(9) To p. 29, n. 4

"CRAS, CRAS." In one of his last letters the late Leo Spitzer pointed out to us that the Roman interpretation of the crow's (or raven's) cry as "Tomorrow, tomorrow" had found its way into medieval literature, here, however, acquiring that menacing connotation which we encounter in Geoffroy Tory and—with the accent blunted but not changed—in Sebastian Brant. In his *Libro de buen amor* (J. Cajador y Franco, ed., Madrid, 1913), lines 1529 ff., Juan Ruiz, Archpriest of Hita (fl. 1343), refers to the black raven (*cuervo negro*) as the "Friend Tomorrow" (*amigo cras*) of Death, and Death himself addresses the reader as follows:

> *Señores, non querades ser amigos del cuervo,*
> *Temed sus amenazas, non fagades su ruego.*
> *El bien que far podierdes, fazedlo oy luego, luego,*
> *Tened que* cras *morredes, ca la vida es juego.*
> *El bien que farás* cras *palabra es desnuda.*

("Sirs, do not seek to be the raven's friends; fear his threats but do not do his bidding. The good you can do, do it today, at once; believe that you must die *tomorrow*, for life is a gamble. The good that you will do *tomorrow* is an empty word.")

Geoffroy Tory and Sebastian Brant retained this negative interpretation; but Alciati, acting under the influence of the classics, reassociated the crow's "Tomorrow, tomorrow" with Hope.

(10) To p. 30, *fig. 11*

THE CAGED BIRD AS A SYMBOL OF HOPE. The tentative explanation of this symbol as "Hope for Liberation" has been documented and splendidly elaborated upon in two articles by I. Bergström: "The Iconological Origins of *Spes* by Pieter Brueghel the Elder," *Nederlands Kunsthistorisch Jaarboek*, VII, 1956, pp. 53 ff.; and "Den fångna fågeln," *Symbolister I* (*Tidskrift för Konstvetenskap*, XXX), 1957, pp. 13 ff.

(11) To p. 33, n. 9

THE HOODED FALCON AS A SYMBOL OF HOPE. This symbol has been explained, with the aid of emblem books where the hooded falcon illustrates the phrase "Post tenebras spero lucem" ("I hope for light after darkness"), by J. G. van Gelder and P. Borms, *Brueghel's zeven deugden en zeven hoofdzonden*, Amsterdam and Antwerp, 1939, p. 27. This important monograph, published at the beginning of the war, is difficult of access in this country even now.

(12) To p. 33

THE EARLIEST POST-CLASSICAL REPRESENTATION OF PANDORA IN PERSON. A representation of Pandora opening the box, which possibly antedates Rosso's drawing (*fig. 16*), is found in one of six tapestries based on Petrarch's *Trionfi* and preserved in the Kunsthistorisches Museum at Vienna: *The Triumph of Death over Chastity* (our *fig. 61*), referred to in Prince d'Essling, *Pétrarque* . . . , Paris, 1902, p. 225 (also mentioned in L. Guerry, *Le*

Thème du "Triomphe de la Mort" dans la peinture italienne, Paris, 1950, p. 216), and illustrated in H. Göbel, *Wandteppiche,* Leipzig, 1923–1934,

First Part, II, Fig. 73, as well as in L. Baldass, *Die Wiener Gobelinsammlung,* Vienna, 1920, ser. CII, 3. In this almost ostentatiously erudite interpretation of the Petrarchian theme the traditional figure of Death is replaced by the Three Fates, and their chariot, drawn by two oxen, is preceded by Pandora, who—releasing "sicknesses" and "plagues"—is here conceived as a harbinger or pacemaker of Death. With her left hand she lifts the lid from a small, cylindrical vessel that she carries in her right, thus allowing a collection of snakes and lizardlike reptiles to escape from it (one snake and one four-footed reptile have already reached the ground).

According to M. R.-A. d'Hulst, to whom we are much indebted for having directed us to the illustrations referred to, the Vienna series is North French rather than Flemish (an opinion shared by R. A. Weigert, *La Tapisserie française,* Paris, 1956, pp. 93 f.), and he agrees with us in doubting the existence of any Italian model. As for the date, everyone admits that the series belongs in the first half of the sixteenth century, and M. d'Hulst believes, as does Göbel, that it was executed "tout au début du XVIᵉ siècle." The *terminus ante quem non* is, of course, the year 1508: it was only after

61. Pandora in a Triumph of Death over Chastity

62. MASTER Z. B. M. (PROBABLY AFTER DOMENICO DEL BARBIERE): *Pandora-Ignorantia*

the publication of Erasmus' *Adagiorum Chiliades* that Pandora could be shown opening a small, portable pyxis.

(13) To pp. 34 ff., *figs. 16, 19, 22–24*

PANDORA, BLINDNESS, AND IGNORANCE. The hypothesis that Rosso's Pandora drawing (our *fig. 16*) was originally connected with the fresco known as *L'Ignorance chassée* in Rosso's Galerie François Premier at Fontainebleau finds support in an unusual etching by the Master Z. B. M. (*fig. 62*), dated 1557 and perhaps designed by Domenico del Barbiere (born at Florence but active at Troyes and Fontainebleau from 1537 to 1562). This Franco-Italian print (for which see D. and E. Panofsky, "The Iconography of the Galerie François Ier at Fontainebleau," *Gazette des Beaux-Arts,* ser. 6, LII, pp. 113 ff., particularly pp. 161 ff. and fig. 58) vividly illustrates the close connection that, in the milieu of Francis I and Henry II, was felt to exist between the Pandora motif and the Ignorance theme. A woman, richly attired and sporting a very complicated hairdo, haltingly approaches a receptacle and, like Pandora, opens its lid. But she differs from all or most other Pandoras in three important respects. In the first place, she releases from the receptacle (which, exceptional for so early a date, is an elaborate casket rather than a pyxis, dolium, or vase) neither a swarm of evils spreading all over the world (as is the orthodox, Hesiodian version) nor a throng of good things escaping to heaven and thus lost to mankind (as is the Babrian version illustrated in our *figs. 38* and *39*), but a strange mixture of both—an idea rampant in France from about 1540 (cf. below, p. 151 f.): from the casket emerge not only symbols of evil (four snakes and two bats) but also symbols of learning and wisdom, viz., a written document and three big books that, as is indicated by their inscriptions, embody the literary heritage of Rome, Greece, and the ancient East. In the second place, the figure is blind: the fingers of her left hand, in pulling down the lower lids of her eyes, reveal that these eyes have neither irises nor pupils; from which we must infer that the woman has acted "unseeingly"—that is, *allegorice,* unwittingly—rather than

under the impulse of willful curiosity. In the third place, her uncomprehend-
ing action, liberating the forces of good together with those of evil, redounds
to the benefit of humanity, though not to hers: unbeknownst to herself, she
has set in motion the powers of light that drive away the creatures of darkness. These powers of light are personified in the female figure on the left,
distinguished from the blind protagonist by an eager look, a simpler attire,
and a coiffure not unlike a modern ponytail swept upward by an imaginary
breeze; all of this characterizes her as a personification of "Intelligent
Thought" (see Cesare Ripa, *Iconologia, s.v.* "Pensiero"), and she is indeed
lighting and vigorously blowing upon a lamp, symbol of Wisdom, Vigilance,
and True Teaching (see Ripa, *ibidem, s.v.* "Sapienza," "Vigilanza,"
"Zelo"). On the right, a third bat and a goat-horned demon flee in disorder.
In the sky, the sun-god, encircled by the zodiac and preceded by Lucifer, the
herald of dawn, is ready to cross the border between night and day, pointing
his finger at Aquarius, the sign of January, which month, needless to say,
marks the beginning of the "Ascent of the Sun" after the winter solstice, thus
spelling the beginning of a new year and a new era.

The etching of 1557, then, goes even further in incorporating the Pandora motif into an allegory of "Enlightenment" than Rosso would have
done had he indeed inserted it into his *Ignorance chassée.* The print confronts
us with a Pandora cast in the very role of Ignorance—or, to put it the other
way, with an Ignorance behaving like Pandora but, unlike her, bringing
about, as an unseeing instrument of all-seeing Providence, an "âge des
lumières" from which she herself is forever excluded.

The iconographical significance of blindness as a symbol of ignorance
and other moral and/or intellectual defects has been discussed, on a much
broader basis than is possible within the framework of a monograph on
Pandora, in an excellent article by W. Déonna, "La Cécité mentale et un
motif des stalles de la Cathédrale de St. Pierre à Genève," *Zeitschrift für
Schweizerische Archäologie und Kunstgeschichte,* XVIII, 1958, pp. 68 ff.

(14) To pp. 40 f., *fig. 20*

"Ex utroque Caesar." For the Greek roots of this concept, see now E. H. Kantorowicz, "On Transformations of Apolline Ethics," *Charites; Studien zur Altertumswissenschaft (Festschrift Ernst Langlotz)*, Bonn, 1957, pp. 265 ff.; cf. also O. Brendel, *Gnomon*, xxx, 1958, p. 391. Professor Kantorowicz called our attention to the fact that a medieval glossator of Justinian's *Institutiones*, Pierre de Belleperche (d. 1308), comes even closer to the final formula (the coiner of which is still unknown) than does the basic text: "Optime concluditur, si utrunque tempus habeat gubernare [Imperatoria maiestas], ideo oportet quod sciat *ex utroque*" (Petrus de Bellapertica, *In libros Institutionum*, Lyons, 1536, p. 29). Two nearly identical emblems in which the motto *Armis et Litteris* is illustrated by a Minerva holding shield and spear in one hand, book and olive branch in the other, was pointed out to us by Professor K. L. Selig: Juan de Solórzano Pereira, *Emblemata centum*, Madrid, 1653, and Andrés Mendo, *Principe perfecto y ministros ajustados . . . en emblemas*, Lyons, 1662, here p. 95.

(15) To p. 52, n. 28, *fig. 38* (cf. also pp. 149 f. and *fig. 62*)

Pandora's Box Containing both Good and Evil. This conflation of the Hesiodian and the Babrian versions, suggested by the ambivalent character of the gifts bestowed upon Pandora by the gods and facilitated by the assumed connection of her pithos with the two pithoi at the Gates of the Palace of Jove (pp. 49 ff., *figs. 25–27*), seems to be of French origin and occurs in writing from about 1540. In *Les Emblèmes de Maistre André Alciat mis en rimes Françoys*, Paris (Wechel), 1540, p. 169, the emblem *Spei Simulacrum* (illustrated by the woodcut reproduced in our *fig. 12*) is explained as follows:

> *Ce tonneau ou ie seetz, faict rapport de l'histoire*
> *Dont Hesiode a faict excellente memoire.*

Car lorsque du tonneau vertus au ciel volerent,
Et que grands maulx vrgens parmy le monde allerent.

Very shortly after, the same idea was expressed in *Pandora Jani Oliverii Andium hierophantae,* a Latin poem (preceded by a *Pandorae Argumentum*) which was composed by Jean Olivier, Bishop of Angers from 1532 to 1540, and pointed out to us by Professor H. van de Waal (first edition, Lyons, 1541; second edition, Paris, 1541; third edition, with French translation by Guillaume Michel dict de Tours, Paris, 1642). Here Jupiter is said to have presented Pandora with a pyxis wherein he has enclosed the Virtues as well as all the Vices ("pixidem in qua virtutes ac omnia vitia incluserat, dono dat"). When the box was opened, the "diseases, the plague, death, and all the other evils" began to wreak havoc among mankind while the Virtues fled to heaven—"except only for Hope, who alone had remained inside, and up to this day rebels and strives to get out." This passage is particularly noteworthy in that it explicitly designates Hope as a Virtue; and in his moralization of the story (for which see below, pp. 154f.) the good bishop even invests her with a distinctly ecclesiastical halo: "Thus Hope, compounded of all the Virtues, is left to us; without her no religion could exist, and the end of all human activity would justly be deemed futile and vain." ("Spes ergo nobis ex omnibus virtutibus perfecta, relicta est, sine qua religio nulla constaret, & omnium operationum humanarum finis inutilis, atque inanis, merito haberetur.")

(16) To pp. 58 f.

PANDORA IN THE POEMS OF JOACHIM DU BELLAY. In his review of our book (*Art Bulletin,* XL, 1958, pp. 159 f.), Professor Henri Peyre reminded us, in the gentlest possible way, of a grave sin of omission and, *in litteris,* assisted us in atoning for it. While we had quoted du Bellay's beautiful sonnet from the *Antiquitez de Rome,* in which Pandora is used as a simile for the Eternal City, we had overlooked the fact that she is also compared, in a graceful octastich entitled "Pandorae nomen aptius fuisse Faustinae" ("By

rights Faustina should have been called Pandora"), to the poet's enchant-
ingly beautiful, capricious, and somewhat sinister mistress, of whom we
know no more than that she was a Roman and made him, in alternation,
blissfully happy and utterly miserable (*Joachimi Bellaii Andini poematum
libri quatuor*, Paris, 1558, fol. 37; in a selection from these poems, edited
and translated by Thierry Sandre under the title *Les Amours de Faustine*,
Amiens, 1923, p. 60):

> *Qui tibi Faustinae, mea lux, nomen dedit, iste*
> *Dixisset Pandora aptius et melius.*
>
> *Munera namque Deos in te omnia congessisse*
> *Ostendunt dotes corporis atque animi.*
>
> *Et tu etiam ex oculis, tanquam de pixide aperta,*
> *Omnia depromis seu bona, sive mala.*
>
> *At mihi te erepta, mi qua sine vivere durum est,*
> *Spes, o me miserum, nulla mihi remanet.*
>
> *(Whoever called Faustina thee, my light,*
> *He should have better christened thee Pandora.*
>
> *For as thy gifts of mind and body show,*
> *The gods compounded all their boons in thee;*
>
> *And from thine eyes, as from the open box,*
> *Thou canst produce all things, both good and bad.*
>
> *For me, alas, bereft of thee without*
> *Whom life is harsh, not even hope remains.)*

It will be noted that a subtly chiastic symmetry exists between this
octastich and the sonnet in the *Antiquitez de Rome*. The very city that, in du

Bellay's words, "locked long in store . . . all that doth feede our spirits and our eies,/ And all that does consume our pleasures soone," had given birth to the beautiful and clever sorceress to whom he says: "And from thine eyes, as from the open box,/ Thou canst produce all things, both good and bad." But while he glorifies the "antique ruines" in living French, he addresses the living woman in Catullian Latin.

(17) To pp. 63 ff., *fig. 29*

"Eva Prima Pandora." It seems to have been in the French Renaissance that the interpretation of Pandora as a pagan Eve was revived from patristic sources (see above, pp. 11 ff.), and it is perhaps no accident that the man apparently responsible for this revival was a humanistically minded theologian rather than a secular scholar or poet: the same Jean Olivier whose *Pandora,* first published in 1541 (that is to say, about eight years before the presumable date of Jean Cousin's *Eva Prima Pandora*), has been referred to on p. 152. Almost immediately before his eulogy on Hope, as quoted above, Olivier writes what follows: "Atqui in hac Pandorae fabula sensus alius altior, & abstrusior subest, qui a Mosaicis mysteriis non multum abhorrere videtur: produnt enim sacrae literae protoplastos serpentino quodam astu instigatos diuinitatem affectasse, esse deo similes concupiuisse, dicente eis serpente: Eritis sicut dii scientes bonum, & malum, si de vetito scilicet ligno comederent: ipsos vero diuinas prohibitiones contemnentes, diuinumque mandatum transgressos, in eas, quas nunc videmus calamitates, & se, & nos posteros suos praecipitasse. . . . Atqui Eua in sacris literis morsu pomum vetitum aperuit, quo morsu mors in orbem terrarum irrupit. Sic Pandora pixidem contra diuinum praeceptum aperuit. Vnde mala omnia, & infinitae calamitates eruperunt, & miseros mortales innumeris cladibus affecerunt, prisca foelicitate cum suis virtutibus (Spe tantum relicta) coelos repetente." In English this reads: "Underlying this fable of Pandora there is hidden another, more elevated and recondite significance, which does not seem to differ very much from the Mosaic mysteries: for Scripture has it that the Protoplasts, instigated by the cunning of the serpent, aspired to divinity and desired to be like unto God, the serpent telling them that they would be like the gods, knowing good and evil, if they would eat from the forbidden tree; and that they, disdainful of the divine prohibition and transgressing the command of God, precipitated themselves and us, their offspring, into the calamities that we now experience. . . . Eve in Scripture opened the forbidden fruit by her bite, by which death invaded the world. So did Pandora open the box in defiance of a divine injunction, whereby all the evils and infinite calamities broke loose and overwhelmed the hapless mortals with countless miseries, whereas the original happiness with its virtues reverted to the heavens, Hope only remaining."

Visually, the equation of Pandora with Eve—and, consequently, of Epimetheus with Adam—is expressed in a pair of rather attractive Spanish wood statuettes preserved in the collection of the Conde de las Infantas at Granada and kindly brought to our attention by Professor Harold E. Wethey: Conde de las Infantas, "Dos Escolturas del Greco?," *Archivo español de arte*, xvii, 1945, pp. 193 ff., our *fig. 63*. These two statuettes, obviously inspired by Dürer's famous engraving B.1 of 1504, so closely resemble the traditional renderings of the Fall of Man that they have been published as "Adam" and "Eve" in the essay just mentioned. Yet the very fact that the head of the male figure is covered with a kind of Phrygian cap and that its right hand gingerly holds a sealed vase—both motifs incompatible with the Garden of Eden— suffices to prove that the so-called Adam is in reality Epimetheus (the artist followed, not surprisingly, the "Philodemus-Erasmus" tradition according to which it is left to the improvident brother of Prometheus to open the fateful vessel) and that the so-called Eve is in reality Pandora. Señor Xavier de Salas had already come to the same conclusion in an article published in the last issue of the *Archivo español de arte*, 1961, pp. 297 ff. We are indebted to him for sending us an offprint of this article before our second edition went

63. Epimetheus and Pandora
Spanish wood statuettes

to press. The photographs reproduced in *fig. 63* were kindly supplied by
Professor Wethey.

(18) To p. 64, n. 15

Nude Personifications Reclining in Front of a City Prospect. For
this motif, cf. a most informative study on Ludwig Refinger's *Allegory of the*

Roman Empire in the Municipal Museum at Ratisbon (Regensburg): E. Simon, "Eine Allegorie des Römischen Reiches, 1539," *Antike und Abendland,* v, 1956, pp. 93 ff.

(19) To p. 67, *fig. 32*

A VENETIAN PARALLEL TO BONASONE'S ILL-BODING PANDORA IN BOCCHI'S "SYMBOLICAE QUAESTIONES." One of the rare representations of Pandora in Italian art, dating from the third quarter of the sixteenth century, is found on the ceiling of the second staircase in the Libreria Vecchia in Venice; see the article by Nicola Ivanoff, "Il Ciclo allegorico della Libreria Sansoviniana," scheduled for publication in *Arte antica e moderna,* IV, 1961. Standing on the left of an Apollo Playing the Lyre and displaying her vase, she forms the counterpart of an *Invidia,* so that both figures must be assumed to bear unfavorable implications. Pandora's inclusion may well be due to the artist's or his adviser's familiarity with Bocchi's *Symbolicae Quaestiones,* which seems to have exerted a considerable influence on mythological and allegorical painting in Venice at the time (cf. N. Ivanoff, "Il Sacro ed il profano negli affreschi di Maser," *Ateneo Veneto,* CXLV, 1961, pp. 1 ff.).

(20) To pp. 71 ff., *fig. 33*

CALLOT'S "CREATION AND DESCENT OF PANDORA." Professor Jan G. van Gelder convincingly suggested that the inordinately large number of classical divinities attending the creation of Pandora in Callot's print might be connected with the fact that the passage from Pliny quoted above, p. 9, was known in the Renaissance in a deviant version, based upon either a corruption in some manuscript or an early typographical error, in which the number of these divinities is increased from twenty (XX *numero*) to thirty. This deviant version is transmitted by Carel van Mander, *Het Leven der oude Antijcke Schilders,* Haarlem, 1604, fol. 65 v.: in describing Phidias' relief on the base of the *Parthenos,* van Mander speaks of *"dertich* Goden."

(21) To pp. 79 ff., *fig. 37* (cf. also pp. 102 ff., *fig. 53*)

EPIMETHEUS SUBSTITUTED FOR PANDORA. In addition to the Spanish statuettes just mentioned, Sébastien le Clerc's engraving (pp. 79 f., *fig. 37*), and Henry Howard's decoration in the house of Sir John Soane (pp. 102 ff., *fig. 53*), the "Philodemus-Erasmus" tradition also seems to have been followed by Jean-Baptiste Claude Robin (1734–1818), one of whose ceilings in the Hôtel de Montholon at Paris is described as representing Justice overcoming the evils released from Pandora's box in such a manner that "Epiméthée renferme l'Espérance au fond de la Boîte." For this description (pointed out to us by Professor John R. Martin), see J. Locquin, *La Peinture d'histoire en France de 1749 à 1785*, Paris, 1912, p. 238.

(22) To p. 82, *fig. 39*

BONASONE'S ENGRAVING B. 144. Our interpretation of this print as a straight illustration of Babrius finds welcome support in the fact that a homespun but literal copy of it was used to illustrate a versified paraphrase of Babrius' fable itself in *Fabulae centum ex antiquis auctoribus delectae et a Gabriele Faerno Cremonensi carminibus explicatae*, Rome, 1564, fol. 94. Gabriello Faerno's paraphrase, found on fol. 33 v. and entitled *Spes*, reads as follows:

> *Bona universa Juppiter coegerat*
> *In dolium; idque sane opertum sedulo*
> *Mortali amico deinde commendaverat.*
> *Is gestiens, quid intus esset, visere,*
> *Cum operculum amovisset, in caelum ilico*
> *Cuncta evolaverunt: spes modo haesit in labro:*
> *Hinc in bonorum sola defectu omnium*
> *Mortalibus spes alma numquam deficit.*

("Jupiter had assembled all goods in a vat; this, properly sealed, he had entrusted to an eager friend who was a mortal. Fervently desiring to see what might be inside, this friend removed the lid, and at once all the goods escaped to heaven; Hope only remained in the vessel. Hence, while all the goods have left them, mortals never lack the comfort of hope.")

(23) To p. 86

A DERIVATIVE OF THE PANDORA STORY IN EIGHTEENTH-CENTURY SWEDEN. What may be called the "Pandora gap" in the visual arts between 1676 (*fig. 37*) and 1775 (*fig. 40*) is filled, after a fashion, by an etching after François Boucher, executed by Quentin-Pierre Chedel (*fig. 64*). It is found in one of the most curious books in history, brought to our attention and made accessible to us by Dr. Carl Nordenfalk: *Faunillane, ou l'Infante Jaune, Conte,* Badinopolis [Stockholm], 1741, plate facing p. 26 (our *fig. 64*). Composed by the famous Swedish statesman, patron, and dilettante, Count Carl Gustaf

64. QUENTIN-PIERRE CHEDEL (AFTER FRAN-
ÇOIS BOUCHER): *The Pensive Princess Opening the Vase*

Tessin (1695–1770), this fascinating hybrid between surrealist fairy tale and *roman à clef* was published, anonymously, in only two hand-corrected copies but is now accessible in a bilingual facsimile edition: S. G. Lindberg, *Carl Gustaf Tessin och flickan från Fånö*, Malmö, 1955. Pandora's role is played by the beautiful Princesse Pensive (who describes herself as "dissimulée et curieuse"), a lady miraculously assembled and enlivened (almost as Galatea was by Pygmalion) by the Prince Percebourse. Married to this prince by the Fée Envieuse, she produces a little girl called Faunillane (after the island of Fånö, here facetiously translated "l'Isle des Faunes"), later known as the Infante Jaune because she always wore a robe of gold lined with black. When this child has grown into a beautiful maiden two malevolent characters, the Fée Lutine and the Sorcerer Gros-Sourcils, attempt to engineer an undesirable match between her and the Prince des Coudes; but the Fée Envieuse, assisted by her friend, the Fée Robinette, prevents this plan by imprisoning Lutine and Gros-Sourcils in a "verre rempli d'une eau de couleur de syrop capillaire," which is deposited on a window sill in Robinette's "Steel Palace." Here the two "enverrés" would have remained forever had not the Princesse Pensive paid a visit to Robinette. The prisoners begin to dance within their glass vessel so as to overthrow it and thus to arouse Pensive's curiosity. In this they succeed. Overcome by her "natural curiosity," Pensive opens the vessel and "puts her nose into it in order to observe at close range such a marvelous thing." No sooner do the Sorcerer and the Fée Lutine sense the approach of their liberty than they profit by it, and from this time they wreck the universe more than ever.

Boucher, it must be admitted, utterly failed to do justice to the surrealist quality of this tale and went so far as to invest the glass opened by the Princesse Pensive with a fatal resemblance to a chamber pot.

(24) To pp. 86 f., n. 5

ARTEMISIA. At first glance a signed painting by S. P. Tilman (1601–68 or 1670), sold at Christie's on April 4, 1949 (No. 140), and brought to our attention by Dr. Horst Gerson, might also seem to represent Artemisia. A richly attired woman is shown opening a big vase that releases neither good nor evil spirits but nothing at all; and on her lap are seen, besides a jewel box and a rope of pearls, a crown, a scepter, and a goblet. But all these objects seem to be sliding down, and the left hand of the figure holds an enormous tulip, apparently of a rare variety. All this, as well as the daring décolleté of the heroine, is not concordant with the faithful widow of King Mausolos. The tulip would rather seem to allude to the notorious "tulipomania" that was rampant in Holland in the first decades of the seventeenth century and resulted in a major financial catastrophe when the States-General, in April, 1637, legalized debts contracted by irresponsible speculators in tulip bulbs. If so, Tilman's painting might be interpreted as a *Vanitas* picture conceived with special reference to the dire results of this tulip craze, and the very point of the big vase would be the fact that it is empty. It may be noted that Tilman was active at Utrecht from about 1639 to about 1646, when the effects of the disaster were still acutely felt, and that the style of his painting agrees with this period of his activity.

(25) To p. 102

A LOST PANDORA CYCLE IN THE ROYAL PALACE AT MADRID. Professor George Kubler called our attention to an extremely important but ill-starred cycle of frescoes on the ceiling of the principal reception room ("Pieza ochavada") in the Royal Palace (Alcázar) at Madrid. Planned and supervised by no less illustrious a master than Velázquez, they were executed, from April, 1659, by three minor painters: a Spaniard, Francisco Carreño; an Italian, Angelo Michele Colonna; and the Spanish-born son of an Italian immigrant, Francisco Rizi (originally Ricci). One of the murals was damaged by rain shortly after and had to be entirely repainted; and the whole cycle was destroyed by the famous fire of 1734.

Fortunately, Antonio Palomino has left us a fairly circumstantial description published exactly ten years before the final disaster: *El Parnaso español pintoresco* . . . , Madrid, 1724, reprinted in F. J. Sánchez Cantón, *Fuentes literarias para la historia del arte español,* IV (Siglo XVIII), Madrid, 1936, pp. 178 f. According to Palomino, the cycle comprised five scenes, the third and fourth conceivably united in one picture (the text is not absolutely unequivocal on this point). First (by Carreño): Vulcan displays to Jupiter the beautiful statue of Pandora that he has produced on the former's orders; his workshop is seen in the background. Second (by Colonna): all the gods, "enthroned on clouds," endow Pandora with their gifts; the composition would seem to have been derived, directly or through the engraving in de Marolles' *Tableaux* (*figs. 35, 36*), from Callot's etching (*fig. 33*). Third (by Rizi): Jupiter presents Pandora with a "riquisimo vaso de oro," destined to be her dowry and to seduce Prometheus. Fourth (also by Rizi): Pandora offers this vase to Prometheus while little Cupid and Hymenaeus, the god of marriage, appear in the distance; but Prometheus, "a wise and circumspect man," refuses both Pandora and her gift. Fifth (begun by Carreño, finished by Rizi, but repainted by Carreño after the above-mentioned rain): Epimetheus, unmindful of his brother's warnings and of the "afflictions, discomforts, and other things attendant upon marriage," yields to Pandora's blandishments and marries her.

If Palomino's description is complete, the cycle would thus not have included the climactic scene, the opening of the vessel. May we assume that Velázquez considered mankind to be sufficiently punished by the *aflicciones y desasosiegos* of marriage as such?

(26) To pp. 105 f., *figs. 45, 55*

THE SQUARE BOX. That the nineteenth century began to think of Pandora's box as rectangular rather than round (the only earlier exception from this rule being the print discussed on p. 149 and reproduced in *fig. 62,* which is unique in every other respect as well) is documented by the fact—pointed out to us by Professor Jan G. van Gelder, who also provided the photograph reproduced in *fig. 65*—that a classical sardonyx, showing a young woman pensively examining the contents of a little square jewel box, was automatically interpreted and illustrated as *Pandore* in *Tableaux, statues, bas-reliefs et camées de la Galerie de Florence et du Palais Pitti . . . avec des explications par [Antoine] Mongez*, III, Paris, 1802, pp. 49 f. (engraving by Claude-Louis Masquelier, known as "Masquelier Fils," after Jean-Baptiste Wicar).

The real subject of the gem may be Eriphyle, the sister of Adrastus, contemplating the fateful necklace by means of which Polyneices bribed her into persuading (or forcing) her husband, Amphiaraus, to join the "Seven against Thebes"; the dire consequences of this war may be alluded to by the hooked spear, difficult to explain in a mere genre scene. It may be noted that on the famous Lecce vase, where Polyneices is shown in the act of offering the necklace to Eriphyle, the precious object is being taken out of a very similar box (A. Furtwängler and K. Reichhold, *Griechische Vasenmalerei*, II, Munich, 1909, No. 66).

65. Claude-Louis Masquelier (after
Jean-Baptiste Wicar): *"Pandora"*
(probably *Eriphyle*)

(27) To p. 106, *fig. 54*

THE BOX AS A MERE ATTRIBUTE. A *Pandora* by Odilon Redon, datable 1908–09, owned by Mr. Alexander M. Bing and illustrated in *Odilon Redon; An Exhibition of Paintings and Pastels, February 9–March 9, 1959*, New York, No. 18, p. 31, is, like that by Jean-Pierre Cortot and others, not much more than a female nude holding a box before her breast. The shape of the box (square but having a rounded lid) somewhat resembles that in Rossetti's composition of 1869–71 (*figs. 56* and *67*), which Redon might have known from reproductions and which would not have failed to impress him.

66. GIOVANNI BATTISTA TIEPOLO: *"Pandora"*

(28) To p. 107, *fig. 55*

A "Pandora" by Giovanni Battista Tiepolo. Professor Justus Bier called our attention to a washed pen drawing by Giovanni Battista Tiepolo in the Kupferstichkabinett at Berlin (*fig. 66*, photograph supplied by Professor Bier). Were it not for the fact that the drawing is inscribed *Pandora*, the figure would be as unidentifiable as the heroine of William Etty's colossal canvas (*fig. 55*) would be if taken out of context. We are confronted with an alternative: either the Berlin drawing is a sketch made in preparation of

67. Dante Gabriel Rossetti: *Pandora*

a *Creation of Pandora* after the fashion of Callot, Diepenbeeck, etc.; or the inscription, which seems to have been added *ex post facto,* is arbitrary.

(29) To p. 108, *fig. 56*

A WATER COLOR BY DANTE GABRIEL ROSSETTI IN PRINCETON (*fig. 67*). This piece, very close to the drawing of 1869 (Marillier 281) and obviously made in preparation of the Graham-Butler painting of 1871 (our *fig. 56*), was brought to our attention by Professor Ernest T. DeWald, who also provided the photograph here reproduced.

(30) To p. 109

A DESPAIRING PANDORA BY WALTER CRANE. In *College Art Journal,* XVI, 1957, pp. 259 ff., Mr. D. Loshak deplores our omission of a water color of 1885 by Walter Crane that, in the artist's own words (W. Crane, *An Artist's Reminiscences,* New York, 1907, p. 276, illustration facing p. 145), shows "the mythical lady after the fatal box has been opened—which I had represented as a marriage coffer [viz., an enormous *cassone,* its corners guarded by sphinxes]—she having cast herself on the lid after the evils had escaped. Through the pillars of the porch is seen a stormy, lurid sunset, and the gleaming curves of a river, barred by the dark forms of cypresses bent before the wind." We are glad to fill this lacuna now.

(31) To p. 118

PANDORA IN SPANISH LITERATURE BEFORE CALDERÓN.

1. In Francisco López de Úbeda's *La pícara Justina,* Medina del Campo, 1605 (Biblioteca de Autores Españoles, XXXIII, E. Fernández de Navarrete, ed., Madrid, 1950, pp. 47 ff., particularly p. 53), the heroine maintains that being poor is of itself no reason for shame and proves her point by twisting the story of the "goddess" Pandora's endowment by the Olympians to suit her purposes: "Pues, ¿ no sabes, pluma mía, que la diosa Pandora fué pobre, y por serlo tuvo ventura, y aun acción a que todos los

dioses la contribuyesen galas, cada cual la suya? . . . Si juntamente con ser yo pobre fuera soberbia, tuviera por gran afrenta el llamarme pelona, como también la misma diosa tuvo por afrenta que se lo llamasen, cuando, por haber sido pobre y soberbia, la deplumaron y pelaron toda los mismos dioses que la habían dado sus ricas y preciosas plumas, y por afrentoso nombre la llamaron la pelona o la pelada. Y de ahí ha venido que a algunos pobres hidalgos, que de ordinario traen la bolsa tan llena de soberbia cuan vacía de moneda . . . los llaman pelones, porque son pobres pelones como la diosa pelada." ("Don't you know, my dear quill, that the goddess Pandora was poor, and, because she was, she had good fortune, and it even happened that all the gods granted her their finery, each one his own? . . . If I were not only poor but also proud, I would consider it a great affront to be called threadbare, even as the goddess herself [Pandora] considered it an affront to be so called when, because she was poor and proud, she was completely plucked and fleeced by the very gods who had given her her rich and precious plumage, and who gave her as an insulting name 'the poor one' or 'the fleeced one.' And that is why certain poor hidalgos, who ordinarily have their purses as full of pride as they are empty of money . . . are called poor men, because they are poor like the fleeced goddess.")

2. An even more confused account of the Pandora myth, in which her fateful vase or box is replaced by an equally Freudian and perhaps even older symbol of lurking evil, the cave, is found in Baltasar Gracián's *El criticón* (M. Romera-Navarro, ed., I, Philadelphia, 1938, pp. 375 ff.). Here "woman," impelled by her inquisitive levity (*curiosa ligereza*), opens a fatal cave (*fatal caberna* or *fatal cueva*) in which all evils are imprisoned. No name is mentioned, and the hope motif is omitted.

We owe these two references, as well as the translation of the passage from *La pícara Justina*, to Professor Willard F. King.

Index

Index

References to illustrations are indicated by an asterisk following the page number.